airfare
SECRETS
EXPOSED

Sharon Tyler & Matthew Wunder

Universal Information Corporation Publishing Co.

AIRFARE SECRETS EXPOSED - The How-To/Resource
Guide To The Absolute Lowest Fares On The Market.

Copyright © 1994
by Sharon Tyler & Matthew Wunder
1st Edition
Printed in the United States of America
ISBN: 1- 881999-26-2

Publisher's Cataloging in Publication
(Prepared by Quality Books, Inc.)

Tyler, Sharon.
Airfare secrets exposed: the how-to /resource guide to the absolute
lowest fares on the market / written by Sharon Tyler and Matthew
Wunder.

p. cm.
Includes biographical references.
Preassigned LCCN: 93-61753
ISBN 1-881999-26-2
1. Airlines--Rates. 2. Air Travel--Directories.   I. Wunder,
Matthew.   II. Title

HE9783.5.T95 1994   387.7'12
                                                QBI93-22549

Printed and bound in the United States of America
10 9 8 7 6 5 4 3 2

WARNING-DISCLAIMER

ACKNOWLEDGEMENTS

If this book could read and speak, it would quote and personify Tennyson by saying, "I am a part of all whom I have met." *Airfare Secrets Exposed* is a compilation of information from many wonderful people who donated their time, expertise and excitement.

Special Thanks to: Toni Carpenter, the expert in the air courier business and editing; Jon Valencia - for his editing expertise, Mark Weiss, for professional advice and Renee Rolle-Whatley for her production and publishing know-how.

Cover design: Renee Rolle-Whatley & Gary Whatley
Interior design: Matthew Wunder

TABLE OF CONTENTS

INTRODUCTION TO
AIRFARE SECRETS EXPOSED

This book will save you a great deal of money on air travel. You will now have a resource guide which enables you to quickly understand and locate airfares that will save you hundreds, if not thousands, of dollars off the regular published prices. You will be traveling to exotic locations for a fraction of the cost of flying as a regular passenger. You will be flying on commercial airlines with others who will have paid 20% - 100% more for the seat next to yours.

You are about to join a small and exclusive group of people who have discovered the secret art of flying inexpensively. We believe you will never want to pay full price for an airline ticket again!

WHO READS
AIRFARE SECRETS EXPOSED?

You would be surprised; we were. When this book was in the, "that would be a fun idea stage," we anticipated our readership to be fixed income people who otherwise were not able to travel -- students! Wrong! The profiles on the people who read obscure information to obtain the lowest airfare are often the same people who are in the financial position to not worry about how much they pay.

So why are people with the financial means to call up their travel agent and buy the first price quoted so enthusiastic about saving money on airfare? Answer: Obtaining the cheapest airfare is considered an art form and/or a thinking person's way of competing. We have spoken to hundreds of people who have either purchased our book or listened to our lecture. The common thread amongst all of our readership is a certain indescribable victorious feeling when they know the passenger sitting next to them paid three times the amount for the same seat.

THE
FREE LANCE
AIR COURIER

INTRODUCTION TO THE FREE LANCE AIR COURIER

An **air courier,** also known as a **free lance air courier** or simply **courier,** is a person who accompanies time-sensitive business cargo that is checked on board an aircraft as excess baggage. In more simplistic terms, an air courier is a person that accompanies freight from one point to another so that the freight can clear customs along with the person. A free lance air courier is just that: free lance. The courier can go on as few or as many trips as he or she wants. A free lance courier is not hired as an employee. He or she is considered an independent contractor for only the time period that they are accompanying the packages. Couriers travel as regular passengers on a plane and accompany freight in name only; they do not sit in the freight belly of the plane. The term "freight" is a generic term that can denote any type of package.

A **courier company** is a wholesale or a retail courier service. Courier companies are responsible for handling express mail on a contract basis for major air freight forwarders and express companies. Simply put, they guarantee the delivery of freight by a certain time; usually the next day, except in the case of the Far East, where it is usually second day service.

The courier company purchases an economy ticket on a regular commercial airline, uses the passenger luggage space for shipping their customers' cargo, and lets you, the free lance air courier, accompany the cargo for a heavily discounted rate. In other words, the freight is treated like it is the personal baggage of the courier. It is cleared on the spot the same way anyone else's baggage would. This is why you are usually giving up your luggage space.

The freight is guaranteed to get through customs immediately and on to the client much more quickly. If a business or individual were to send the package unaccompanied, it would be treated as any other freight sent internationally, and would be inspected and cleared in a customs house before it could be delivered to the receiving party.

The package you accompany for the courier company actually clears customs with you and your personal belongings; cutting the customs' clearing time down dramatically. As you can see, the courier companies need couriers.

Free lance air couriers are not employed by a courier company. Free lance air couriers are considered independent contractors who are performing a one-time service for the courier company. This service is merely accompanying the freight while riding comfortably to the country of your choice for a price far below that paid by other passengers. In exchange for your services, the courier company pays a portion of your ticket and you pay the rest. Your fare still ends up being far below the cost of a retail ticket.

To illustrate the reasons that air courier companies exist and the benefits to you, let us look at two different scenarios in which a company could ship a package both via regular air freight and via courier. Assume the following:

ABC Inc., a multi-national widget manufacturer, needs to send a "special widget" to it's Copenhagen office for a Danish customer. The customer is willing to pay three times the regular price for this "special widget" if it can be delivered from the U.S. within 24 hours.

Now lets take the following two scenarios as an illustration:

Scenario 1

ABC Inc. uses the **air freight** facility service of an airline (Does **not** use a courier company). ABC Inc. would have to get its packages to the airport at least 3 or 4 hours before the flight took off so that the airline could load it into the freight belly of the plane.

Upon arrival in Copenhagen, ABC's package would immediately be put into a **bonded warehouse**. A bonded warehouse is simply a warehouse where everything that has not been cleared by customs is stored. Finally, the package would be taken out of bond and sent to a **customs clearance agent**.

This can be a very time consuming process, because, if something goes into a bonded warehouse, it has to be cleared sequentially. (Who knows how many packages, are ahead of ABC Inc.'s and how many customs agents are working that particular day).

Eventually the package clears the customs warehouse and awaits pickup by a delivery service or representative of the Copenhagen office of ABC Inc.

Scenario 2

"X Courier Company" in Los Angeles is offering next day service to Copenhagen. They guarantee their customer, ABC Inc., that their "Special Widget" will be delivered within 24 hours.

ABC Inc. sends their widget to "X Courier Company," who in turn prepares it for shipping. "X Courier Company" can either send it on as it is or co-load it with another one of their packages going to Copenhagen on the same flight.

Co-loading or consolidating packages is the process of putting several different smaller packages into one very large bag and sending the smaller packages as one. (The courier companies are changing to large heavy duty plastic bags with their logo on them- these are used 1 or 2 times, then thrown away).

"X Courier Company" would then prepare a manifest (a list of everything contained in the shipment). The manifest tells the customs agent what is in the shipment. It is a very important document.

"X Courier Company" arranges for you, the courier, to accompany the freight to Copenhagen. The freight (the widget) is treated like the personal baggage of the courier. It is cleared on the spot; immediately, the same way anyone else's baggage would. ABC Inc. now has the widget to give to their Danish customer with time to spare.

Courier companies offer their clients the following advantages:

- The quickest means of delivering a package internationally.

- A predictable and definite time of arrival.

- Safety from damage and theft that can occur in some bonded warehouses. The package you carry for the courier company actually clears customs with you and your personal belongings.

- The courier company guarantees the safe and timely delivery of their customer's package.

AIR COURIER
QUESTIONS ANSWERED

Am I qualified to be a free lance air courier?

You must be 18 to 21 years or older (depending on the courier company). You must have a valid passport. Some companies also require a drivers license and major credit card.

If you are flying into a country which requires a visa, you will need to obtain one prior to departure.

You must be in good health. In certain rare cases, couriers may have to put the bags on a baggage cart in the customs hall.

Do I have to be a U.S. citizen?

Generally, nationality does not matter. You must have a U.S. passport, multiple entry visa or green card.

Is there a dress code?

As a courier, you will be expected to dress in a clean, neat and professional manner. Dress standards reflect the company's image. Casual attire (shorts, racy or suggestive T-shirts and "unconventional" hair styles) or intoxication of any kind are not permissible. Blue jeans are allowed by some courier companies if they are clean, without holes and unfaded. You should look like someone an immigration official would let into his country. You must act in a professional manner at all times. Courier companies have to maintain good relations with the airlines and customs officials.

What will I be carrying?

You are **accompanying** courier bags that weigh up to 80 lbs. each. These bags are checked as passenger baggage and travel in the baggage compartment of the aircraft. Normally, the only thing you actually **carry** is the document pouch which contains the manifest, the all important courier instructions, baggage claims and other documents pertaining to the courier shipment. This pouch usually weighs under 5 lbs. and should be kept with you at all times.

The types of items that are usually taken by a courier are:

• Commercial papers: stock certificates, banking transactions, legal documents or anything where the original is required.

• Video tapes: news stories could be sent by satellite, but this is very expensive, so companies have them hand carried.

• Machine parts.

• Anything that needs to get somewhere very quickly.

The packages that are couriered are from companies that make their money legally. Courier companies work from a large list of clients that they ship for all the time. They obtain releases from their clients stating their shipments contain nothing illegal. The individual shipments are inspected prior to being manifested, by bonded personnel. Custom officers also know that the courier does not ever touch the shipment. So, in answer to the question that we hear most often, " No, you are not smuggling drugs."

How do I get my tickets and check-in for departure?
Different courier companies have different procedures for giving you your tickets, manifest and instructions. Frequently you will meet a representative at a predetermined meeting place at the airport and receive all the necessary documentation. Another procedure for checking in is to go directly to the courier company, which is typically within a few miles of the airport. You will check in there, be given your airplane tickets and then be chauffeured over to the airlines. Generally your driver will load the cargo onto the plane for you.

Note: Drivers are sometimes late, up to an hour, so don't panic! It is a good idea to keep the phone number of your courier company with you in case you need to call.

Two words of advice if you plan on flying courier more than once:

- Check in (phone call) with the courier company 24 hours prior to departure, if requested to do so.

- Keep all of your time commitments with the courier company.

How long can I stay on my trip?

The length of a courier trip varies. Some courier companies have predetermined return dates which cannot be negotiated while others are within a particular time span of anywhere from four days to six months. If a courier company says you must return on "x" date, they mean "x" date, be careful of pushing too much - there are other couriers. Courier companies that predetermine your length of stay have gauged the minimum length of stay an "average" courier would be willing to go. The courier companies would love it if couriers would fly to country "x" for them, use the airport restroom

and get on the next flight back. Of course, the courier companies know that most couriers are unwilling to do that, so the courier companies set their lengths of stay to a reasonable amount of time in order to attract free lance couriers.

What are my instructions for returning?

In some cases, you will receive a return flight instruction sheet when you originally depart along with your return ticket: don't lose them. In other cases, you will meet a representative at your destination city to receive your return tickets (much like you did for your departure). Most courier companies require you to be in your departure city 24 hours prior to departure. Also, make sure to make your check-in call; flight arrangements can change! To return to the U.S.A. you must have your re-entry papers.

How do I clear customs?

Clearing customs varies from country to country. Regulations will be spelled out on the information sheet the courier company will give you along with your tickets. In some countries, a representative will meet you and clear the documents, in other countries you will need to clear the documents by yourself.

What are the typical rules and responsibilities of the air courier?

There are a set of terms that you must agree to abide by - these are common sense rules. You must "report for duty" a day before the flight. You must keep your security/manifest papers in your sight at all times. Your baggage allowance is for carry-on luggage only - no check-in luggage is allowed unless you make arrangements with the courier company in advance. Generally, tickets are not refundable.

Some companies may refund a portion of the ticket, check this out when you book your flight. You can get trip insurance. You will be asked to sign a contract for international flights.

How is payment handled?

In order for the company to feel secure in that they have a courier for their flight, they are going to want payment as soon as possible. Each courier company will let you know their payment requirements.

How do I pay?

You can usually pay with a money order, certified check and, sometimes, a personal check. Some courier companies will take a credit card as well.

Are their any security deposits?

Because couriers are given such low airfares, some courier companies require a fully refundable security deposit to insure that the courier will return as agreed. They are 100% refundable, assuming you comply with your simple duties and follow all regulations. There are no tricks; courier companies make too much money shipping freight to bother hassling over security deposits. Make sure to reclaim it.

Besides the ticket price and security deposit, what other costs might there be?

You can expect the usual departure taxes. Check with your destination country for how much this will be and put it aside. Don't spend it.

What if I don't follow through on my responsibilities?

You have effectively denied yourself the opportunity of ever flying so cheaply again with the same courier company, and many others - they network. You may also lose your security deposit, and even your return ticket.

Where can I travel as an air courier?

The courier business changes constantly. If a route is profitable for a courier company, it will continue. As new markets open up, so do new courier routes. Right now, Africa is the only continent you can't get to directly via air courier from the U.S. (From the U.S. you can fly courier to London then catch another courier flight onto Africa).

Are all courier flights international?

Generally, yes. The U.S. domestic market for free lance air couriers has diminished drastically. We have listed one agency that has begun domestic courier service from L.A. to New York.

How should I plan a courier trip?

You can choose one of three ways. You can pick a destination with approximate departure and return dates, then call the courier companies. They are usually very helpful. A second method is to pick a destination and take whatever dates they have available. The third way is for the adventurous traveler; you just select your travel dates and take whatever destination is available.

Can I make a reservation in advance?

Yes. Most courier companies book flights up to two months in advance. Sometimes, a last minute cancellation will occur and you can get an even greater deal - but you must be able to leave on a moments notice. The closer the deadline, the better the deal. Some courier companies do not offer last minute deals though, so do not assume they do.

If you know that you want to book for a heavily traveled time of year, find out what day the "books" open and call in on that day and make a reservation. Different companies have different deadlines. If you book far enough in advance, you may get the exact flight of your choice.

Are the flights round-trip?

For most flights, you will be a courier in both directions. You are given a set length of stay for these round trip courier flights. Some flights have a variable return time in which you choose a return time within certain parameters. **Whether you are expected to bring back a package with you on the return or not, you will be given a round-trip airline ticket unless you are told otherwise by the courier company.**

Can I make vacation plans as a courier?

You can make vacation plans around courier schedules 98% of the time. If your flight is changed by the courier company, your trip most likely will be the day before or the day after the original date.

If your flight is delayed or canceled by the airline, you are entitled to the same treatment and/or compensation as any other passenger with respect to cancellations and delays.

Can two or more people travel on the same day?

Yes and no. Generally, only one courier is needed by any one particular courier company at a time. But ask! It is possible that two different courier companies will be sending their couriers on the same flight. It is possible for two people to go to the same destination on the same day, but, for different courier companies and on different airlines. Either way, we recommend that you use a courier booking agency for your convenience when traveling with another person since they have access to several courier company schedules.

The most common and easiest way for two people to travel courier is to book you on one flight and your companion on the next flight out to the same destination; usually the next day.

Another way is for one person to book as a courier, while the other person pays for a regular ticket (or a consolidator ticket) - as a couple, you've still saved a lot!

Am I allowed to take carry-on luggage only?

Well, usually. Less is more to the seasoned traveler. Having all your belongings in your possession can save you huge amounts of time when passing through customs. If you can't travel with just a carry on, you can also bring a small backpack, a large tote, a purse or camera case. But, if you insist on more than two carry-on bags and/or checking in luggage, we have a few suggestions for you:

- The courier company may not necessarily need all of their allotted baggage space, ask your courier company if they will allow you some extra space.

- Ask the reservation agent at the ticket counter if you can check an extra bag at no extra cost. If the plane is not full, they may be willing to check an extra piece.

- You can also pay an "excess baggage" fee to the airline to check it on board. (Call ahead for prices and check with the courier company for their policy.)

Because of the size restrictions, you will want to pack well: coordinate your clothes, bring fewer "outfits," bring wash and wear clothes. Don't pack too light; make sure to take enough clothes. For toiletries, take small sample sizes.   You will be surprised how many outfits and accessories you can fit into a big carry-on bag which is still under airline carry-on regulations. Remember, 95% of all courier flights are not to the wilds of Borneo - you will be able to purchase an acceptable substitute for anything you have forgotten.

AUTHOR'S NOTE: We highly recommend you invest in a **Jesse LTD. Flight Tote**. It doubles as a shoulder bag with a detachable strap or simply unzip the back panel to reveal adjustable, padded shoulder straps to carry it as a backpack. It is perfect for the freelance air courier because it is the **maximum allowable size carry-on** which also allows for overstuffing. You'll be glad you bought it. ($70 includes shipping and handling. Black, Maroon, Gray, Blue). You can order one from:

Jesse Ltd. 305 W. Crockett, Seattle, WA 98119
or call 1-800-274-3048

Are there restrictions on my duty free allowance?
No. You are allowed to bring $400 of duty free purchases into the United States - as long as they are in compliance with U.S. Customs. The next $1,000 is charged a flat 10%. If you plan to shop internationally, do not ship your packages back to yourself. If you ship your purchases back, you are allowed only $25 per day per address. Instead, if you need extra space, you can mail your used clothing to yourself.

Can I earn frequent flyer mileage credits?
Most likely. Check with the airline prior to departure. Some will give you frequent flyer mileage, some will not. It pays to ask. When you are checking in, tell the reservation agent you want your flight credited to your frequent flyer account, give them your airline ticket/stub, say nothing else and wait for a response.

Can I upgrade my ticket?
No. You cannot upgrade a courier flight; you must be

willing to fly in economy class. However, if the flight is not full, you may be able to switch your seat to another one in the same class of service.

Generally, how much can I expect to save?

Depending on when you book a flight, you can expect to save 50% and up off of what a normal full fare would cost. However, more people being aware of courier flights has driven courier fares up in price.

How can I get the best deal?

Ask if there are any last minute specials. Typically, courier companies offer last minute fares only to those people who have flown with them before.

How do courier companies price their tickets?

Courier companies must purchase their tickets from the airlines. The price depends on the agreement between the courier company and the airline. Their ticket cost may fluctuate depending on the season.

Ticket prices fluctuate depending on desirability and destination and competition. Six months from now the prices may not be the same. Call around to find out who is offering what and for what price.

Interestingly enough, the courier companies have found that if they charged no money at all, people did not show up for their flight.

Am I really paying for an airline ticket?

No. You are buying a courier trip. The ticket was purchased by the courier company and it belongs to them. Your name may or may not be on it.

If your name appears on the ticket, make sure to ask that the flight mileage be credited to your frequent flyer account.

How do I decide between using a courier travel agent or dealing directly with a courier company?

The main booking agencies are located in New York. The advantages to agencies are: you get a broader range of destinations, they often have last minute flights (which are substantially cheaper), and sometimes they have free flights. A courier travel agency can also book connecting flights, arrange hotels and car rentals and other travel needs. Another big advantage to a courier travel agency is that they are more likely to arrange for two people to fly on the same flight because they book for several courier companies.

The disadvantages of not going directly through the courier company and using a courier travel agency include having to pay a fee for their services (they often mark up their flights to cover their service) and they may charge a membership fee. Only if you are planning to make a lot flights, should you join a courier membership program in advance. Always join at the last possible point, because your membership is only good for one year from the date of purchase.

When calling a courier company directly, tell them you
are a free lance air courier and you would like to book a
flight. All you have to do is say where you want to go
and pay your money.

Do courier companies make other travel arrangements?

Courier companies are not travel agents, so do not rely
on them to make other arrangements for you. On the
other hand, a travel agency specializing in courier flights
can make other travel arrangements for you.

COURIER COMPANIES & COURIER TRAVEL AGENCIES DIRECTORY

There are a few books out on the market solely devoted to flying as a free lance courier. Our book has the most comprehensive listing of VALID courier companies anywhere. We do not pad our directory with companies that do not use free lance couriers. We do not want you wasting your time calling obsolete phone numbers. However, courier flights and destinations rapidly change. For this reason, we recommend that you join **The International Association of Air Travel Couriers** for their updated newsletters, Fax-On-Demand-Service and On-Line courier flight availability. They update their information on a daily basis and provide current fare information, which airlines fly to each destinations, the person(s) to contact at the courier company, minimum and maximum length of stays and all other pertinent information that a perfect-bound "book" cannot keep current. (see Travel Resources We Recommend)

Usual destinations for the courier companies have been included as a simple guide to aid you in your decision making of which courier company or courier travel agency to call first. Please keep in mind that some destinations close, while others open. Because prices, airlines flown, and length of stays change all the time, we generally do not include them.

Courier travel <u>agencies</u> are denoted by an (*).

CHICAGO

Halbart Express
147-05 - 176th Street
Jamaica, N.Y. 11434
(718) 676-8279
(718) 676-8189
Destinations: London & Frankfurt.

IMS Courier Service
2821 E. Commercial Blvd. Suite 203
Fort Lauderdale, Florida 33308-3459
Destinations: Jamaica.
(305) 771-7545
(305) 771-6730 (FAX)

HOUSTON

International Bonded Courier (IBC)
3050 McKauhan Street
Houston, TX 77032
(713) 821-1900
Destination: Mexico City.

Now Voyager
74 Varick Street, Suite 307
New York, NY 10013
(212) 431-1616
(212) 334-5243 (FAX)
Destination: London.

LOS ANGELES TO NEW YORK

*1st World Travel/Silverflight
11952 Wilshire Boulevard.
Los Angeles, California 90025
(310) 207-6353
(818) 881-5117
Destinations: L.A. to N.Y. & L.A. to Hong Kong.
Ask for Gale

LOS ANGELES

Excalibur International Couriers
6310 West 89th Street
Los Angeles, CA 90045
(310) 568-1000
Destination: Asia. Book through Way to Go.

IBC-Pacific
1595 East El Segundo Boulevard
El Segundo, CA 90245
(310) 607-0125

(310) 607-0126 (FAX)
(415) 697-5985 (recorded information line for LA flights)
Destinations: Tokyo, Hong Kong, Singapore, Bangkok, Taipei, Seoul, Sydney, Manila.

Jupiter Air (MICOM America)
6733 Sepulveda Blvd. #170
Los Angeles, CA 90045
(310) 670-5251
(310) 649-2771(FAX)
Destinations: Hong Kong , Seoul & Singapore.

Midnite Express International Couriers
930 West Hyde Park Boulevard
Inglewood, CA 90302
(310) 672-1100
(310) 671-0107 (FAX)
Destination: London.

Now Courier
619 South New Hampshire Avenue
Los Angeles, CA 90005
(310) 671-1200
(213) 252-5070
1st World Travel/Silverflight currently books their courier flights.

POLO Express
9100 South Sepulveda, Suite 108
Los Angeles, CA 90045
(310) 410-6822
(310) 641-2966 (FAX)

Destinations: Hong Kong, Sydney, Melbourne, London, Bangkok, Tokyo.

SOS International Courier
8715 La Tijera Boulevard
Los Angeles, CA 90045
(310) 649-6640
(310) 649-1214 (FAX)
Destination: Mexico City.

***Way To Go Travel**
6679 Sunset Boulevard
Hollywood, CA 90028
(213) 466-1126
(213)466-8994 (FAX)
Destinations: Hong Kong, Bangkok, Singapore, Kuala Lumpur, Penang, Djakarta, Sydney, Melbourne and Mexico City.

MIAMI

A-1 International
6930 NW 12th Street
Miami, FL 33126
(305) 594-1184
(305) 594-2967 (FAX)
Destination: Venezuela.

DTI
940 10th Street #2
Miami Beach, FL 33139
(305) 538-1616

Destinations: London, Madrid, La Paz, Sao Paolo, Montevideo, San Salvador, Santiago, Rio De Janeiro, Buenos Aires, Caracas, Guatemala City, Lima, Guayaquil, Quito, Mexico City.

Halbart Express
2471 NW 72nd Avenue
Miami, FL 33122
(305) 593-0260
(305) 593-0158 (FAX)
Destinations: London, Madrid, Rio De Janeiro, Mexico City.

Line Haul Services
formerly Carrier A Bordo (CAB)
7859 NW 15th Street
Miami, FL 33126
(305) 477-0651
(305) 599-2002 (FAX)
Destinations: Lima, Caracas, San Salvador, Santiago, Rio, Guayaquil, Quito, Guatemala City, Buenos Aires, Bogota, La Paz, Panama City.

Martillo Express
585 East 49th Street
Hialeah, FL 33013
Destinations: Guayaquil.

Skynet Worldwide Courier Network
4405 NW 73rd Avenue
Miami, FL 33166
(305) 477-0996
(305) 477-0998 (FAX)

SOS International Courier
8715 La Tijera Boulevard
Los Angeles, CA 90045
(310) 649-6640
(310) 649-1214 (FAX)
Destination: Mexico City.

Trans-Air System
7264 NW 25th Street
Miami, FL 33122
(305) 592-1771
(305) 592-2927 (FAX)
Destinations: Guatemala City, Quito, Santiago, Buenos Aires.

NEW YORK

*Able Travel & Tours
18 East 41st Street
New York, NY 10017
(212) 779-8530
Destinations: London, Paris.

Air Facility
153-40 Rockaway Boulevard
Jamaica, NY 11434
(718) 712-0630
(718) 712-1574 (FAX)
Destinations: Buenos Aires, Caracas, Santiago, Rio De Janeiro, Montevideo.

Courier Network
295 7th Avenue
New York, NY 10001
(212) 691-9860
(212) 675-6876
(212) 92905186 (FAX)
Destination: Tel Aviv (six days a week).

*Discount Travel International (DTI)
152 West 72nd Street
New York, NY 10023
(212) 362-8113
(212) 362-5310 (FAX, call first)
Destinations: Europe, South America, Hong Kong.

East-West Express
P.O. Box 30849
JFK Station
Jamaica, NY 11430
(516) 561-2360
(516) 568-0477 (FAX)
Destination: Johannesberg, Sydney, Bangkok.

Halbart Express
147-05 176th Street
Jamaica, NY 11434
(718) 656-8279
(718) 656-8189
(718) 244-0559 (FAX)
Destinations: Brussels, Budapest, Berlin, Dusseldorf,
Frankfurt, Hamburg, Stuttgart, Rome, Milan,
Amsterdam, Stockholm, Madrid, London, Copenhagen,
Paris, Prague, Zurich, Helsinki, Moscow, St. Petersburg,

Kiev, Tallin, Riga, Santiago, Mexico City, Johannesburg, Tokyo.

Jupiter Air, Ltd. (MICOM America, Inc.)
160-23 Rockaway Boulevard
Jamaica, NY 11434
(718) 656-6050
(718) 656-7263 (FAX)
Destinations: Hong Kong & Singapore.

Micom
Building # 14 JFK International Airport
Jamaica, NY 11430
(718) 656-6050
Destinations: Hong Kong, Singapore.

*Now Voyager
74 Varick Street, Suite 307
New York, NY 10013
(212) 431-1616
(212) 334-5243 (FAX)
Destinations: Amsterdam, Brussels, Copenhagen, Frankfurt, Helsinki, Madrid, Milan, Paris, Rome, Stockholm, London, Buenos Aires, Santiago, Montevideo, Rio De Janeiro, Caracas, Mexico City, Hong Kong, Singapore, Bangkok, Tokyo, Sydney, Johannesburg.

POLO Express
160-23 Rockaway Boulevard
Jamaica, NY 11434
(516) 371-6864
Destinations: London, Singapore.

Rush Courier
481 49th Street
Brooklyn, NY 11220
(718) 439-9043
Destination: San Juan.

SOS International Courier
8715 La Tijera Boulevard
Los Angeles, CA 90045
(310) 649-6640
(310) 649-1214 (FAX)
Destination: from New York to Mexico City.

World Courier, Inc.
137-42 Guy R. Brewer Boulevard
Jamaica, NY 11434
(718) 978-9552, 978-9400
(718) 276-6932 (FAX)
(718) 978-9408 (recorded message line)
(800) 221-6600
Destinations: Brussels, Milan and Mexico City.

SAN FRANCISCO

*Focus on Travel
155 Bovet
San Francisco, CA 94402
(800) 722-3246
(415) 571-0323
Books for IBC Los Angeles office; will help set up
accommodations at destination cities.

Jupiter Air, LTD (MICOM America, Inc.)
#90 South Spruce Ave. Suite I
South San Francisco, CA 94080
(415) 872-0845
Destinations: Hong Kong, Singapore, Manila.

POLO Express
811 Grandview Drive
South San Francisco, CA 94080
(415) 742-9613
(415) 742-9614 (FAX)
Destinations: Hong Kong, Bangkok, London.

*UTL Travel
320 Corey Way
South San Francisco, CA 94080
(415) 583-5074
(415) 583-8122 (FAX)
Destinations: Hong Kong, Singapore, Manila, London.

*Way To Go Travel
1850 Union Street, Suite 6
San Francisco, CA 94123
(415) 292-7801
Destinations: Bangkok, Hong Kong, London.

ARGENTINA

DHL International S.A.
H. Yrigoyen 448
Buenos Aires, Argentina
011-54-1-331-3217
Destination: Buenos Aires to Miami.

AUSTRALIA

POLO Express
P.O. Box 457
Mascot NSW, 2020 Australia
011-61-2-319-6011
Destinations: Sydney to Auckland and Los Angeles.
May be able to book through U.S. office.

Jupiter
P.O. Box 224
Mascot NSW, 2020 Australia
011-61-2-317-2230
Destinations: Sydney to Auckland and London.

Bridges Worldwide
P.O. Box 242
Spit Junction NSW, 2088 Australia
011-61-2-969-5472
Destination: Sydney to London.

TNT Express Worldwide
280 Coward Street
Mascot NSW, 2020 Australia
011-6102-317-7717
Destination: Sydney to Auckland.

CANADA

F.B. On Board Courier Service
10225 Ryan Ave., Suite 103
Dorval, Quebec H9P-1A2
(514) 633-0740
Destinations: Montreal to London, Toronto to London.

or

P.O. Box 23641, APO
Vancouver V7B-1X8
(604) 278-1266
Destinations: Vancouver to London and Hong Kong.

Jet Services
2735 Paulus
Ville St-Laurant, Quebec H4S 1E9
(514) 331-7470
Destination: Montreal to Paris.

ENGLAND

Bridges Worldwide
Unit 61/62 G, Building 521
Heathrow Airport
Middlesex TW3-3UJ
011-44-81-759-5040
011-44-81-759-8069 (FAX)
Destinations: London to Bombay, Malta, Sydney, Tokyo,
New York, Los Angeles, Boston, Newark and Miami.

*Courier Travel Service
346 Fulham Road
London, SW 10 9UH
England
011-44-71-351-0300
Can book through New York office.
Destinations: London to Miami, New York, San
Francisco, Harare Zimbabwe, Mauritius Islands, Nairobi
Kenya, Hong Kong, Tokyo, Rio de Janeiro.

F.B. On Board Courier
01144-0753-680280
01144-680424 (FAX)
Destinations: Montreal, Toronto.

Polo Express
208 Epsom Square
London Heathrow Airport
Hounslow, Middlesex TW6 2BL
011-44-81-759-5383
011-44-81-759-5697 (FAX)
Can book through New York office.
Destinations: London to several cities throughout
Europe, the Middle East, Africa, Asia and the U.S.

Jupiter Air Couriers
Jupiter House
Horton Road
Colnbrook, Slough SL3-OBB
011-44-75-368-9989
Destinations: London to Sydney.

Line Haul Express
Building 200, Section D, Enfield Road
London Heathrow
Middlesex TW6-2PR
011-44-81-759-5969
011-44-81-759-5973(FAX)
Destinations: London to Hong Kong, Sydney.

FRANCE

Jet Services Roissy
3 Batiment 3416, Module 700
Route du Midi, 95707 Roissy
France
011-33-14-862-6222
Destinations: Paris to New York and London.

Halbart Express
39-39 rue Broca
5th arrondissement, Paris
France
011-33-45-87-32-30
Destination: Paris to New York.

GERMANY

Line Haul Express
GEB, 453,
60549 Frankfurt, Germany
011-49-69-69793260
Destinations: Frankfurt to Hong Kong, Hong Kong to Tokyo, Sydney, Bangkok, Manila and Taipei.

GUATEMALA

LINE HAUL SERVICES
7a Avenida 14-70 Zona 13
Aurora 1 Guatemala
011-502-2-31-2086
Destinations: Guatemala City to Mexico City, Panama City, Miami.

HONG KONG

Jupiter
Room 1701, Tower Number 1
33 Canton Road
Kowloon, Hong Kong
011-852-7-351946
Destinations: Hong Kong to Bangkok, Sydney, Tokyo, N.Y., San Francisco Los Angeles, Vancouver, London.

Great Bird Room 1009, Hang Shing Building
363 Nathan Road, Kowloon, Hong Kong
011-852-3-321311
Destinations: Hong Kong to Taipei, Tokyo.

Line Haul Express (Sophia Lai)
Room 2209-B, Tower One
33 Canton Road ·
Kowloon, Hong Kong
011-852-7-352163
Destinations: Hong Kong to Bangkok, Frankfurt,
London, Manila, Taipei, Tokyo, Vancouver, Singapore.

Bridges Worldwide
Room 894, Pacific Trade Center
2 Kaihing
Kowloon Bay, Hong Kong
011-852-3-051412
Destinations: Hong Kong to Sydney, San Francisco,
London, Singapore, Bangkok.

*Courier Travel Service
011-852-305-1413
Destinations: Bangkok, London, San Francisco,
Singapore, Sydney.

JAPAN

Shona International
201 Alcazar, 2-16-3 Higashi Mizuhodai
Saitama Ken 354 Japan
001-81-4-92559150
Destinations: Tokyo to London, Hong Kong, Vancouver.

Jupiter Japan
779-3 Azuma-Cho
Narita, Chiba 286 Japan
011-81-4-76242157
Destination: Tokyo to London

MEXICO

Mex Courier
America 187, San Lucas Coyoacan
Mexico City, Mexico
1-905-689-2944
Destinations: Mexico City to Miami and New York.

NEW ZEALAND

TNT Express Worldwide (New Zealand)
6 Doncaster Street
Mangre, Auckland, New Zealand
011-64-9-275-0549
Destinations: Auckland to Los Angeles, Honolulu, Seattle, San Francisco, Vancouver, Sydney, London, Frankfurt.

Polo Express
P.O. Box 73150, Auckland International Airport
Auckland, New Zealand011-64-9-275-1263
Destination: Auckland to Sydney.

SINGAPORE

Air United
5002 Beach Road, #03-64 E
Golden Mile Complex
Singapore 0719
011-65-2945954
Destinations: Singapore to Los Angeles, San Francisco,
Bangkok, Tokyo, London.

TNT Travel
1 Shenton Way
Robina House, 18th Floor
1806 Singapore
011-65-2227255
Destination: Singapore to Los Angeles.

OBCC Express
24 New Industrial Road, #05-04
Pei Fu Industrial Building
Singapore 1953
011-65-281-1373
Destination: Singapore to Bangkok.

TAIWAN R.O.C.

Jupiter International
7th Floor, Section 2 #62
Nanking East Road
Taipei 104, Taiwan ROC
011-886-2-551-2198
011-886-2-581-1867 (FAX)
Destination: Taipei to Los Angeles.

THAILAND

Siam Trans International
78 Kiatnakin Building, Bushlane, New Road
Bangkok 10500, Thailand
011-66-2-235-6741
011-66-2-236-1042 (FAX)
Destinations: Bangkok to Singapore, Hong Kong.

Wholesale Courier Company
Bangkok Thailand
011-66-2-255-4614
011-66-2-254-3675 (FAX)
Destinations: Bangkok to Singapore, Hong Kong,
London.

VENEZUELA

A-1 International Courier
Avenida Romulo Gallegos
Edificio Torres de Ugar, Local J - Horizonte
Caracas, Venezuela
011-58-2-239-2041
Destination: Caracas to Miami.

THE
CONSOLIDATORS

INTRODUCTION TO THE CONSOLIDATORS

Airlines know that some of their seats will go empty on certain flights. This is lost revenue for them. In order for them to sell more seats, an airline will take the anticipated number of empty seats and sell them off in bulk at a cost far below any published fare. The person or company that buys these tickets will then mark up the tickets, and sell them to the public or other travel agencies. The public gets a great deal, and the airlines sell tickets that would otherwise go unsold. The person or company that buys these tickets in bulk and sells them for a profit is called a **consolidator**.

For example, a full fare, round trip, coach ticket on ABC Air to Paris costs $1,000. The airline is concerned that they will not sell all their seats, so they sell 100 seats to a consolidator for $250 per seat. The consolidator has the choice to either sell the tickets themselves or sell them to a retail agency, let's say for $350. A retail agency would then mark up a profit and sell to the public, for $450. Travelers get a great bargain at $450 and even a better one at $350 if they can cut out the middle man.

The ticket price, the economy, the demand for the particular destination, and the competition play a role in how full or empty any one particular flight might be and thus, how many consolidator tickets are available. The season plays a factor as well. Off season, (i.e. Fall for many destinations) means lost revenue for the airlines. During these times when there are more seats available, the airlines are more apt to sell their unused tickets to the consolidators.

Airlines are not quick to admit they sell tickets to consolidators. Some airlines will deny they use consolidators when they really do. This is because if their regular passengers were to discover the prices these tickets were being sold at, they would expect the same low rate as well. If you were to call a ticket agent or regular travel agent and ask for their best deal, they still would not be able to compete with consolidator prices.

A friend of ours in the travel industry told us of an amusing story about attending an airline convention. A high ranking official of a foreign airline that will remain anonymous, pontificated how selling to consolidators was unethical, in the worst interest of the airlines and a practice that his airline has never and would never engage in. Our friend still kicks himself for not speaking up and reminding the speaker that just six months prior to this convention, this same airline official approached our friend to buy a block of seats for fifty cents on the dollar.

Some airlines have even set up their own in-house consolidating businesses. Instead of this being a discreet one person operation, some airlines have recognized the need for establishing sophisticated consolidator divisions within their corporation.

Consolidator prices are not a published fare. The computer systems that travel agents use do not list consolidator tickets and not all travel agencies have access to these tickets.

CONSOLIDATOR QUESTIONS ANSWERED

How do airlines choose to whom they sell these deeply discounted tickets?

The airlines sell their tickets in quantity to "high production" travel agencies who can work with volume. These agencies are generally in those cities where flights take off for other continents. These cities are also known as Gateway Cities. Some airlines actually have their own in-house ticket consolidating business.

How much might I save by purchasing a consolidator ticket?

Consolidators price the tickets to what they feel they can get quickly and in large quantities. There is no set formula. During peak season travel, when tickets prices are high, you can expect to save 20-30%. When travel volume is low, all prices become lower and your savings would be less. Often, for one-way flights, consolidator tickets are just a little more than half of a round trip fare (airlines generally charge much more). Tickets that need to be "dumped" in a hurry may be negotiated for pennies on the dollar.

Why wouldn't a traveler want to fly on a consolidator ticket all the time?

Consolidator tickets are a great opportunity and are always worth looking into. However, they are not offered as frequently as regular full fare tickets. Occasionally, discount tickets do not qualify for advanced seating arrangements, and you may end up with the least desirable seat. Generally, consolidator tickets are only good for the issuing airline: if you miss a flight or your flight is delayed, your ticket probably won't be honored on another airline. Also, if you are interested in frequent flyer miles, some airlines do not accept tickets bought through consolidators for their frequent flyer programs.

What are some other restrictions?

Consolidator tickets have "non-refundable" written on them, because they usually have the regular fare printed on them rather than the price you paid (airlines don't want you turning in you ticket for a profit). If you must cancel your flight and want a refund, you'll have to go through the consolidator and/or his agent.

Often a consolidator ticket will have less restrictions on it than promotional fares by the airlines. Even if the price of the consolidator and the promotional ticket is the same, it may be worth it to buy a consolidator ticket.

Are consolidator tickets always coach or can I fly first class?

Most of the consolidator tickets are coach, although you can occasionally find first or business class tickets. First Class and Business Class prices are not as great a bargain either. You cannot usually upgrade a discount ticket by paying a surcharge. If the regular fare is printed on the ticket, (rather than what you paid or just the tax) you might have a chance to do so. Give it a try.

How do I find a consolidator?
We have listed many for you in our directory. Please note that some consolidators will deal only with travel agents and not the general public. You have a choice, you may wish to call the consolidators yourself or, you may wish to contact a travel agent who will search for a consolidator ticket for you. When contacting a travel agency, keep in mind that many do not sell consolidator tickets. Also, remember a travel agent works for money and will most likely tack on a fee for their work.

Another source for consolidator tickets is your newspaper's Sunday travel section. Unfortunately, not all are legitimate. You could actually end up buying a stolen and/or an unauthorized ticket. Let the buyer beware.

How should I pay for my ticket?
When buying your ticket, it's best to use your charge card and pay the finance charge. Think of it as insurance: if your ticket isn't as you like, apply for a refund through your card. Also, make sure you have the actual ticket in your possession before paying for it completely.

CONSOLIDATOR DIRECTORY

The following is a list of agency's that sell consolidator tickets. These agency's offer tickets to different parts of the world. If one agency doesn't have the ticket you want, call another one. Because consolidator destinations change frequently, we do not list the destinations each agency sells. However, the following agency's collectively sell airplane tickets to Africa, Asia, Caribbean, Central America, Europe, Hawaii, Middle East, North America, South America and the South Pacific.

ARIZONA

Cefra Discount Travel (602) 948-5055

Council Travel (602) 966-3544

Panda Travel (602) 943-3383

NORTHERN CALIFORNIA

Aereo (Cut Throat) Travel (800) 755-8747

Air Brokers International (800) 883-3273

All Continents Travel (800) 247-7283

BET World Travel (800) 662-2640

The Budget Traveler (415) 331-3700

Char-Tours (800) 323-4444

Cheap Tickets (415) 896-5023

Council Travel S.F (415) 421-3473

Berkeley (510) 848-8634

Davis (916) 752-8548

Palo Alto (415) 325-3888

Custom Travel (800) 535-9797

Departures (800) 654-1130

Euro Asia Express (800) 782-9625

Global Access (800) 321-7798

Magical Holidays (800) 433-7773

Omniglobe Travel (415) 433-9312

Scan the World (415) 325-0876

Skytours (800) 246-8687

STA Travel (510) 841-1037

Sun Destination Travel (415) 398-1313

Sunco Travel International (800) 989-6017

Sunline Express (800) 786-5463

Travel Time (800) 235-3253

Way-To-Go Travel (415) 864-1995

SOUTHERN CALIFORNIA

Air Brokers International (800) 833-3273

All Continents Travel (800) 368-6822

ANZ Travel (800) 735-3861

Canatours (213) 223-1111

Cheap Seats (800) 451-7200

Cheap Tickets (310) 645-5054

Continental Travel Shop (310) 453-8655

Costa Azul Travel (213) 525-3300

Council Travel (800) 743-1823

H.O.T. Travel (714) 541-2700

La Jolla (619) 452-0630

Long Beach (310) 598-3338

L.A. (310) 208-3551

Magical Holidays (800) 421-8771

San Diego (619) 270-6401

Santa Barbara (805) 562-8080

Sherman Oaks (818) 905-5777

Japan Express (213) 680-0550

Jetway Tours (213) 382-2477

Pacifico Creative Services (800) 367-8833

Rebel Tours (805) 294-0900

South Star Tours (800) 654-4468

STA Travel (213) 934-8722

W.L.A. (310) 394-5126

Supersonic (800) 439-3030

TFI Tours (213) 687-3500

Way To Go Travel (213) 466-1126

COLORADO

Council Travel (303) 447-8101

Fare Deals (800) 878-2929

CONNECTICUT

Council Travel (203) 562-5335

FLORIDA

Council Travel (305) 670-9261
DeTravel (800) 637-9597
Getaway Travel International (305) 444-6647
Gilmore International Travel (800) 228-1777
Guardian Travel (800) 741-3050
Intervac (800) 992-9629
Interworld (305) 443-4929 (800) 331-4456
Lachelle Granholm (407) 582-6297
25 Travel (305) 250-4525 (800) 252-5052
Miami Travel Centre (800) 788-0072
NEWS Travel & Tours (800) 992-9629
Rebel Tours (407) 352-3600
TFI Tours (800) 745-8000
The Smart Traveller (800) 448-3338

GEORGIA

Council Travel (404) 377-9997

Everest Travel (800) 952-7534

GIT/Travel Wholesalers (800) 228-1777

Midtown Travel Consultants (800) 548-8904

Skyway Travel (404) 525-6824

Spalding Corners Travel (404) 441-1164

HAWAII

Asia Travel Service (808) 926-0550

Emerson (808) 537-6996

Fly-On (808) 524-2200

Cheap Tickets (808) 947-3717

Pali Tours & Travel (808) 524-2483

ILLINOIS

Austin Travel (800) 545-2655

Bargain Airfares (800) 922-2886

Compare (312) 853-1144 (800) 343-6974

Council Travel (312) 951-0585

Cut Rate Travel (800) 388-0575

Hobbit Travel (312) 693-8200

McSon Travel (800) 622-1421

Mena (312) 472-5631

Overseas Express (312) 262-4971

Sunbeam Travel (800) 433-3161

Travel Corner (800) 554-6342

Travel Avenue (800) 333-3335

Travel Center (312) 726-0088

Travel Core of America (800) 992-9396

Travnet (800) 359-6388

TFI Tours (800) 745-8000

US Intl Travel & Tours (800) 874-0073

RTC International (312) 853-2700

INDIANA

U.S. International (219) 255-7272 (800) 759-7373
Council Travel (812) 330-1600

KANSAS

Cheap Tickets (800) 377-1000

LOUISIANA

Council Travel (504) 866-1767
RMC/Dixieland (800) 489-4629
Uniglobe Americana Travel (504) 561-8100

MARYLAND

Fare Deals (800) 347-7006
Suburban Travel (800) 466-7954

MASSACHUSETTS

Council Travel -Amherst (413) 256-1261
other locations in Boston, Northeastern University &
MIT
Intrac (800) 873-4687
STA Travel (617) 266-6014
another office in Cambridge

MICHIGAN

AIT (800) 365-1929
Council Travel (313) 998-0200
Travel Charter Int'l (313) 528-3500

MINNESOTA

Council Travel (612) 379-2323
Plymouth Travel (800) 736-8747

MISSOURI

Group & Leisure Travel (800) 874-6608
UniTravel (800) 325-2222

NEW JERSEY

Marcus Travel (800) 524-0821
Rupa Travel Services (800) 438-7872
Worldvision Travel Services (800) 545-7118

NEW YORK

Aerotours Intl (800) 223-4555
Balkan Holidays (212) 573-5530
C & C Travel (800) 767-2747
Consumer Wholesale Travel (800) 223-6862
Council Charter (212) 254-2525
Flytime Tour & Travel (212) 760-3737
The French Experience (212) 986-986-3800
Globe Travel Specialists (800) 969-4562
Great Destinations (212) 832-7212
Homeric Tours (800) 223-5570
Hurtuk (212) 750-1170 (800) 366-8785

Magical Holidays (800) 228-2208

New Frontiers (800) 366-6387

Park South Travel (212) 686-5350

Maharaja Travel (212) 213-2020 (800) 223-6812

RMC (212) 697-6560 (800) 782-2674

STA Travel ((212) 854-2224

another store in Greenwich Village

Travac Tours and Charters (800) 872-8800

Travel Center (212) 947-6670

Travel Travel Consulting (800) 435-9247

Tulips Travel (800) 882-3383

2M Intl Travels (800) 938-4625

Up and Away (800) 275-8001

Wings of the World (800) 835-9969

NORTH CAROLINA

Council Travel (919) 942-2334

Magical Holidays (800) 235-4225

OHIO

American Travel (216) 781-7181
Council Travel (614) 294-8696

OREGON

Council Travel (503) 228-1900
Emmett Travel (800) 742-1000
Pacific Gateway Travel (800) 777-8369
STT Worldwide Travel (800) 348-0886
Unique Travel (800) 397-1719

PENNSYLVANIA

Council Travel (215) 382-0343
Pennsylvania Travel (800) 331-5810
STA/University Travel (215) 382-0343

RHODE ISLAND

Council Travel (401) 331-5810

TEXAS

Airvalue (903) 597-1181
Airfare Busters (800) 232-8783
Carefree Getaway Travel (817) 430-1128
Council Travel (512) 472-4931
EST Intl (713) 974-0521
Katy Van Tours (800) 528-9826
Royal Lane Travel (800) 329-2030

UTAH

Council Travel (512) 401-331-5810

VIRGINIA

Fellowship Travel Intl (800) 446-7667
Trans Am (703) 998-7676
Travel Network (800) 929-1290

WASHINGTON D.C.

Americas Tours (800) 553-2513
C & G Travel (206) 363-9948
Cathay Express Travel (800) 762-8536
Council Travel (202) 337-6464
EZ Travel (206) 524-1977
New Wave Travel (206) 527-3579
Sun Makers (800) 841-4321
Travel Network (800) 933-5963
Travel Team (206) 632-0520

WISCONSIN

Council Travel (414) 332-4740
West Allis (414) 475-9400

CANADA

Pacesetter Travel (604) 687-3083

Vacances Escomptes (514) 861-9090

THE
AIR PASS
PROGRAMS

INTRODUCTION TO THE AIR PASS PROGRAMS

An Air Pass is a "multi-flight coupon book" of discount tickets offered by airlines to travelers who reside in a different country. They may not be called, "Air Pass" per se, but they all are essentially the same.

If you plan to explore a country thoroughly and don't particularly like long bus or train rides, this is a good means of getting about quickly and more economically than buying the tickets individually. This is the airlines' answer to the popular Eurailpass.

In most cases, you must purchase your pass before you reach your destination. Most often an air pass must be purchased in conjunction with an international flight on the carrier from which you are purchasing the air pass. Some airlines will still sell you an air pass if you do not fly internationally with them, but at a higher rate. A few airlines sell the passes through travel agents only. Obviously, the easiest way to purchase one is to contact a knowledgeable travel agent and ask them if there are any air pass programs available for the countries you wish to visit. However, you can book most passes on your own. You will need to know your destinations ahead of time for most air pass programs; though some air passes allow you "unlimited" flights. The starting and ending dates must be set, but the intermediate dates can often be left open. Prices and programs occasionally change.

AIR PASS DIRECTORY

Aero Peru
Visit South America (800) 777-7717
- Six flights in the low season, $999.
- Six flights during the high season, $1,184.
- Each extra flight, $100.
- Flights originate from Miami.
- 45 day maximum.
- Peru and two more South American countries from Los Angeles, $1396.

Aerolineas Argentinas
Visit Argentina (800) 333-0276
- Four coupons, $450.
- Can purchase up to four more coupons at $125 each.
- Purchase in conjunction with international ticket.
- Return to Buenos Aires for connecting flights.
- Coupons cannot be shared amongst travelers.
- All good for 30 days, maximum. Good for any city in Argentina.

Air France
Euroflyer Pass (800) 237-2747
- Travel throughout Europe (CSA, Sabena, Air Inter, Air France routes).
- Seven day minimum, two month maximum.
- Three to nine coupons for $120 each.
- In conjunction with U.S.A. to Paris ticket.
- 100 cities to choose from.

Air India
Discover India (800) 223-7776
- Unlimited flights during a 21 day period, $400.
- May only repeat a city if it is for a flight connection.
- The 21 day period starts the day you take your first trip in India.
- Operates in conjunction with Indian Airlines.

Air New Zealand
Air Pass (800) 262-1234
- Minimum of three tickets for $240.
- Maximum of eight coupons for $600.
- Good for the length of your international ticket.
- Operates in conjunction with Mount Cook Airlines.
- Must stipulate your cities, but not the dates.
- May fly any carrier there, but purchase Pass in the U.S.A.

Air Paraguay
Visit South America (800) 677-7771
- U. S. A. to Paraguay, plus two other cities to which they fly, $1084 (1993).
- Offered during low season of February through October.
- Maximum stay 30 days.

Avianca
Discover Colombia (800) 284-2622
- During low season (January through May and September through November) five stops in Colombia during a 21 day period $142 without stopping at Leticia and San Andres, $220 with Leticia and San Andres.
- Ten stops in Columbia during a 30 day period, $224 without Leticia and San Andres, $325 with Leticia and San Andres. Good all year.
- During high season, five stops within a 21 day period $162 without stopping at Leticia and San Andres, $250 with Leticia and San Andres.

Aviateca
Mayan Pass Fares (800) 327-9832
- Three different cities (Mexico City, Merida, Tikal, $399).
- Start in Guatemala and visit within South America, minimum four coupons, $65 each.
- For some cities, Guatemala City is the point of connection (Belize, San Salvador).

British Airways
Air Pass (800) 247-9297
- Start and finish in London, Birmingham, Glasglow or Manchester.
- Price depends on where you are going.
- Travel within Europe in conjunction with Gibraltor Airways and German Domestic.
- Book and pay seven days in advance.

Canadian Airlines International
Visit USA Fares (800) 426-7000
- Flight must originate from overseas (not from N. America). Prices based on destinations. Better prices than regular fares, but advanced booking fares are often cheaper.

East/West Airlines of Australia
Air Pass (800) 354-7471
- Queensland Pass: Sydney to Cairns with two free stops 480 Australian.
- Sun Air Pass: Sydney to Ayers Rock, Alice Springs to Cairns and Cairns to Sydney (can stop all places between Cairns and Sydney), 649 Australian.
- System Air Pass: East coast, North of Cairns and Tasmania, unlimited, 751 Australian.
- Fly internationally on Qantas.

Faucett, The First Airline of Peru
Visit Peru (800) 334-3356
- Unlimited flights during a 45 day period, $250.
- Good for any city inside Peru to which they fly.
- Prices higher flying internationally on another carrier.
- Visit cities once, except Lima, for connecting purposes.

Finnair
Holiday Pass (800) 950-5000
- Unlimited flying throughout Finland in a 15 day period, $300.

Garuda Indonesian Airways
Visit Indonesia - Air Tickets (800) 342-7832
- Three cities during a five day minimum and 60 day maximum, $300.
- Four cities during a 60 day maximum, $400.
- Ten cities during a 60 day maximum, $1,000.
- Destinations are counted as "cities," not the connecting cities.
- Start at gateway cities of Bali, Medan, Djakarta.
- In conjunction with Merpati Airlines.

Hawaiian Airlines
Hawaiian Air Pass (800) 367-5320
- Unlimited flights in the state of Hawaii.
- Five days, January to June 30, $149; July - December, $159.
- Seven days, January to June 30, $169; July -December, $179.
- Ten days, $219.
- Fourteen days, $259.
- Need picture ID and ticket in order to book.
- Make reservations before you go to the ticket counter.
- Program up for renewal in June 1994.

Iberia Airlines of Spain
Visit Spain (800) 772-4642
- Four segment pass, not returning to the same destination, during a 60 day period, in the Fall or Winter $249; in the Spring or Summer $299.
- Should one of your destinations be a Canary Island, add $50.
- Each additional flight, $50.
- Circle trip (Except if you are going to the Canary Islands, you do not need to return to your original destination).
- Purchase with transatlantic flight.
- Not valid with free flights (i.e.. frequent flyer).

Ladeco Airlines
Visit Chile (800) 825-2332
- Unlimited flights in Northern or Southern Chile within 21 days, $300; child fare, $180 (including Easter Island, $1,080; child fare, $570).
- Unlimited flights throughout Chile within 21 days, $550; child fare, $330 (including Easter Island $1,290; child fare, $680).

Lan - Chile Airlines
Visit Chile (800) 735-5526
- Five cities in Northern Chile or three cities in Southern Chile within 21 days, $300.
- Eight flights throughout Chile within 21 days, $550.
- Unlimited flights to Easter Island within 21 days, $812.
- Unlimited flights to Easter Island and Northern or Southern Chile within 21 days, $1080.
- Unlimited flights to Easter Island and throughout Chile within 21 days, $1290.

Lloyd Aereo Boliviano Airlines
Visit Bolivia (800) 327-7407
- Six cities in a 15 day period, $135.
- May only go to a city once.
- May make changes for an additional fee.

Malaysia Airlines
Discover Malaysia Pass (800) 421-8641
- Five cities in Malaysia's three areas, 40% discount on normal fare.
- Five cities in one of Malaysia's areas (i.e.. the Peninsula) $138.
- Good for 21 days after using the first sector.
- One way round-trip or circle trip in coach class.
- Issued with purchase of one international sector.

Mexicana
Air Pass (800) 531-7921
- Colonial: four cities, $250, additional cities $65 each.
- Beaches: four cities, $360, additional cities, $100 each.
- Interior: four cities, $470, additional cities, $130 each.
- Caribbean: four cities, $450, additional cities, $120 each.
- Two day minimum, 45 day maximum.

Qantas Airlines
Australia Explorer Pass (800) 227-4500
- Minimum booklet of four coupons, $440.
- Including Perth or outer island, $514.
- One way air service, fully open, fully changeable.
- Flights assigned on availability (you may want to have back up flights confirmed).
- Good with any international flight (including frequent flyer!).

Royal Air Moroc
Discover Morocco (800) 344-6726
- Four coupons, $149.
- Six coupons, $199.
- Maximum length, six months.
- Cannot be shared amongst travelers.

Scandinavian Airlines - SAS
Visit Scandinavia (800) 221-2350
- Each one-way flight, $80.
- Good for flights between cities in Sweden, Norway and Denmark.
- You must know your routings, before purchasing.
- Maximum of six flight coupons.
- Fully refundable, if you haven't used any coupons.
- Purchase in conjunction with international ticket.
- May change dates of travel, but cannot change routings without incurring $50 per route change penalty.

South African Airways
Africa Explorer (800) 722-9675
- Each segment priced differently.
- Minimum of four coupons, maximum of eight.
- Minimum stay of three days, max. stay of one month.
- Dates may be left open until first flight, then they must be confirmed.Example: Johannesburg to Durban, to Port Elizabeth, to Cape Town, to Johannesburg, approximately $300.
- Purchase with international ticket. 25 % cancel. fee.

Sahsa Honduras
Mayan World Fare (800) 327-1225
- Minimum of three cities (i.e.. Belize City, San Pedro Sula, Roatan, Tegucigalpa, Guatemala City), $399.
- Maximum five cities.
- Maximum stay 21 days.
- Must be purchased seven days prior to departure.
- Originates in Miami, New Orleans or Houston.
- December 1 through January 15 blacked out.

Thai Airways International
Discover Thailand (800) 426-5204
- Four flight coupons within 60 days, $239.
- Your first flight holding must be confirmed.
- The rest of your itinerary must be set, but the dates may be left open.
- Up to four more additional coupons, $50 each.
- Purchase in the U.S. A.

Trans Brazil
Visit Brazil (800) 872-3153
- Five cities in Brazil, $440.
- Up to two more additional stops, $100 each.
- Maximum of 21 days.
- Must be have an international ticket, on any airline.

Varig Brasilian Airlines
Brasil Pass (800) 468-2744
- Five different cities within a 21 day period, $440.
- Additional flights, $100 each.
- May fly any airline into Brasil.
- Only issued after international ticket has been bought.

DOMESTIC AIR PASS

Kiwi International Airlines
Kiwi Bonus Pack (800) 538-5494

- Six one way tickets between Newark to Orlando, Atlanta and Chicago, $590 ($98 each).
- Tickets good for one year.

CHARTER
FLIGHTS

INTRODUCTION TO CHARTER FLIGHTS

Charter flights are large groups of seats purchased and usually marketed to a particular group of travelers. For instance, a student charter business might offer a flight to Europe for students while some charter operators send planeloads of people living in a cold, winter weather climate to warm, tropical destinations.

Charters can be less than regular excursion fares, but one should compare prices carefully. The upside to charter flights are that they **may** be cheaper than promotional fares or consolidator tickets. Also, charter tickets may be the last cheap ticket available when the airlines are sold out of their promotional fares.

The downside to charter flights are that they do not depart as often as other types of flights and can be sold out quickly. They are also not very flexible in terms of cancellations and departure/return dates. Travel agents are not usually aware of these flights because they are not in their computer system.

CHARTER DIRECTORY

Apple Vacations East
(800) 727-3550

Apple Vacations West
(800) 365-2775

Balair
(800) 322-5247

C and C Travel
(800) 869-2431

Club America Vacations
(800)221-2931

Council Charter
(800) 800-8222

Club Vacations
(516) 424-9600

Funway Holidays Funjet
(414) 351-3553

GWV International
(800) 225-5498

MLT Vacations
(800) 362-3520

Martinair Holland
(800) 366-4655

Nouvelles Frontieres
(800) 677-0720

Skytours
(415) 777-3544

STA Travel
(310) 394-3271

Travel Charter
(313) 528-3500

Way To Go Travel
(213) 466-1126

Welcome Tours
(800) 274-4400

Wings of the World
(800) 634-9464

HIDDEN
AIRFARE TIPS

The following are some simple strategies that will save you a ton of money .

LONDON: AIRFARE HAVEN

It is often cheaper to fly to London and then find a cheap fare from there to some other European, African or Middle Eastern destination than it is to book a flight from the United States. Additionally, last minute (within 48 hours) deals can be incredibly cheap.

The English work system encourages its countrymen to travel. Non-tenured and tenured workers alike, regardless of their job position, are given a minimum of one month of vacation per year. With so many Brits "on holiday," the travel business has become big business in England. Competition and volume have driven the prices to some locations way down. Below are three big discount agencies in London that sell consolidator or other low priced tickets.

Bluewheel Travel LTD.
Tel: 081-202-0111
Fax: 081-202-3839

Bridge the World Travel Centre
Tel: 071-911-0900
Fax: 071-916-1724

Major Travel
Tel: 071-267-4840
Fax: 071-487-2719

BUYING TICKETS ABROAD

Similar to LONDON: LAND OF AIRFARE BARGAINS, purchasing a portion of your ticket abroad can be a great money saver. For example, we flew to Singapore via courier for $350 roundtrip. We took a train to Maylaysia and purchased two roundtrip tickets to a resort island in Thailand called Phuket. We flew Thai Air, (excellent airline), stayed in a five star hotel for five nights, including tours and airport pickup, all for less than $350. Sure, this was a tour price. However, the U.S. Dollar was so strong against their Maylaysian Ringit, we figured that buying a ticket in Maylaysia or any country where our dollar is strong, can easily save a bargain hunter 40%.

SOME SMALLER AND CHEAPER AIRLINES

Deregulation has prompted the launching of several smaller, yet competitive, airlines. It is a matter of speculation whether or not these airlines will survive. However, the bottomline for the consumer are some very low cost alternative fares. These airlines often service routes that the larger airlines charge higher fares for because of the lack of perceived demand to that area.

Reno (800) 736-6247
Kiwi (800) 538-5494
Carnival (800) 437-2110
Mark Air (800) 627-5247
Private Jet (800) 949-9400
Morris Air (800) 466-7747
Spirit Airlines (800) 772-7117
Wings of the World (800) 835-9969
American Trans Air (800) 831-9117

GROUP INCLUSIVE TOURS

Group Inclusive Tours (GIT) are airline seats purchased for a group. They are usually cheaper than full fare prices because they are sold by the airlines in volume to the tour operator.

Sometimes a tour operator cannot fill a tour's seat quota and has too many tickets for a given flight. They occasionally relinquish the extra tickets to travel agencies. The tickets are then sold to individuals at a discounted rate, similar to that of large group purchases. You will find the sale of GIT tickets at some travel agencies, ask your agent if he/she has them available. See Consolidators.

HUB AND SPOKE

The Hub and Spoke concept is based upon the way that airlines centralize their operations to a certain city(s). An airline chooses a city in which to base its mechanics, flight staff and lay-overs, in order to reduce overhead costs. The Hub is the main city, the cities where the airline flies to are the Spokes.

The airlines centralize in order to increase profitability. They organize their flights to go through their Hub city in order to reduce the high expenses of employing people and running operations out of their Spoke cities.

For Example: A ticket on "Acme" Airlines from Los Angeles to Raleigh that stops or connects in Denver (Acme's Hub) is usually less expensive than a direct flight between the two Spoke cities.

The major airlines continue to have direct, non-stop flights for people who wish the convenience and time-savings of non-stop flights and don't mind paying a little more for it.

Occasionally, you will find an airline offering double frequent flyer mileage to passengers flying via the Hub. This is a promotional gimmick that could earn you a lot of miles for a few hours of your time - it's worth checking out.

Look for fares that may be cheaper by flying through an airline's Hub rather than flying directly from spoke to spoke. Check whether it may be cheaper to fly to their Hub, switch planes, and fly onto your destination.

While the Hub and Spoke philosophy was widely accepted in the 1980's, the airlines are now consolidating their hubs. In other words, use it while it lasts.

HIDDEN CITIES

Some cities are cheaper to fly to if you pretend you are going on to another destination. Your ticket might say L.A. to N.Y. with a stopover in Washington D.C. You do not have any intention of going to N.Y. though your ticket says you do. You get off in D.C. and discard the remaining portion of your ticket.

Why? Because if Washington D.C. is a hidden city, (this is just an example and is not necessarily correct) the fare will be less than if you booked a flight from L.A. to Washington D.C. direct. There has even been an entire book written on this subject. The problem is that if your L.A. to N.Y. ticket has you return schedule on that ticket and it does not have a record of your re-boarding the plane in Washington D.C., your reservation will be canceled automatically from the computer.

Some ways around this problem are either to (A) check-in but never get on the plane (tricky to accomplish) or (B) book your return flight on another airline. The problem with (B) is that most good fares are based on a round-trip purchase. Option (C) is to let the airline know that you have gotten off at the stopover for "business or personal reasons" and that you want to make sure that your return flight will not be affected. The reservation operator will bypass the computers' automatic "dump the reservation" command.

This ploy will not work if you have checked baggage. Airlines will not check bags to D.C. with a N.Y. ticket. Also, they will not take off if they are missing a passenger with checked bags. Passenger bags will be off-loaded for security reasons/terrorist considerations.

PROMOTIONAL FARES

Promotional fares are round trip airfares that have some additional restrictions. Restrictions could include: cancellation penalties, minimum or maximum length of stay, non - refundability or advance purchase requirements.

Promotional fares are sparked by an airline's need to promote some new feature such as a new destination, a new airplane or expanded service. Another reason is that sales may be slipping and they want to promote the airline's service to that destination.

You can expect a savings of at least 20%. But, you must be flexible as to when you want to travel. These are often short lived promotions and have many conditions.

Promotional fares are often advertised in the newspaper travel sections. Just browsing through the section may save you money. Travel agents, though, are often informed of a promotional fare before the public is told. If you work with a travel agent ask her/him to keep you in mind for last minute promotional tickets to the destinations you want to visit.

TOUR DISCARDMENT

Often you will see package deals that offer airfare, accommodations, car rentals and various other package perks for less than the best price you were quoted on airfare alone. The reason these tours exist at such a spectacular price is a tour company's ability to buy and sell these vacations in volume. Of course, you may not wish to be part of a tour. What you can do is purchase the package, get the great airfare, discard the other "amenities" and still go for less than booking it all individually.

For example: A seven day tour to Jamaica, including airfare, hotel, car rental and welcome cocktail, costs $700. A round-trip flight to Jamaica costs $850. Even if you do not want or need the full tour package, you save $150 by flying with the tour.

SENIOR AIRLINE COUPONS

Travelers 62 and older are able to buy a book of coupons good for travel both domestically and internationally that are priced well below other published fares

Just like the air pass programs that have one set price for a number of flights, Senior Airline Coupons allow the senior traveler to pay a low set fee and fly to several destinations of their choice.

Call the airline that flies to the destinations you are interested in and ask about their senior program.

FREQUENT FLYER PROGRAMS

INTRODUCTION TO THE FREQUENT FLYER PROGRAMS

Frequent Flyer programs were started by the major airlines in the early 1980's to promote flyer loyalty. They wanted to reward travelers who flew their airline regularly. Today, frequent flyer programs have become an integral part of the airlines ploy to induce customer loyalty.

The major Frequent Flyer programs work much the same way -- for each mile you fly, you earn at least one credited mile. Once you have earned a specified number of credited miles, you turn them in for benefits such as, free trips, upgrades and discounts on car rentals and hotels. The airlines' rewards differ, but it typically takes 20,000 miles for your first free trip within the U.S.'s 48 contiguous states.

Programs have expanded dramatically and often include rewards for the use of "partners" (certain airlines, car rental agencies, hotels, long distance phone companies, Credit cards and same or next day package delivery). Despite the enormous attention the frequent flier programs have generated, only 15% of all frequent flyer mileage earners actually redeem their mileage. This startling fact can be partially attributed to the complicated and often convoluted programs offered by each of the airlines.

FREQUENT FLYER QUESTIONS ANSWERED

How do frequent flyer programs work?

You earn mileage for flights you take on your frequent flyer program. You earn mileage one time only per flight, despite the number of seats you personally purchase. Once you have accumulated enough mileage, you start putting it towards rewards (class upgrades, free tickets, discounts etc.).

How do I get mileage credit?

Simply give the travel agent or airline your frequent flyer number when making reservations and upon checking in at the airport.

Can I pool my mileage with other travelers in the program?

No, only individual accumulations are accepted. Frequent flyer programs will **not** allow you to transfer your miles to another person so that they can pool your mileage with theirs. But, some programs will allow you to transfer **awards** to traveling companions or relatives and United and Northwest will allow you to transfer **awards** to friends. You can transfer trip awards, not mileage.

Who can enroll?

Individuals. Some programs have a minimum age requirement of at least two years of age. Pets or blocked-seat luggage are not enrollable. Some airlines have a corporate program.

How do I enroll?

There are two options: 1. You may call the airline's 800 number or 2. You may fill out the enrollment form at the airport. You'll receive information about the program and your personal ID number in the mail. Almost all of the programs are free.

How many programs should I join?

Join the program of each airline you fly -- even if you don't foresee enough future flights on the airline to get a free trip, you may be eligible for smaller benefits. If the economy section of the plane is full, some airlines will upgrade by choosing "frequent flyers."

For the best returns on your travel mileage, it is worthwhile to "concentrate" your mileage on only a few airlines. This would mean deciding on what programs are best for you, and then doing most of your business with those airlines.

If I join more than one program, do I get credit on all programs that are partners with the one I fly?

No, mileage credit is good for only one program per ticket.

What if I open accounts on many airlines, but never use them?

Many programs require you to fly within the first nine months of enrollment or your account will be closed. Concentrate your mileage accumulation on one or two airlines.

I've already flown on a particular airline but haven't enrolled, can I still get credit?

Typically, no. Usually mileage credit accumulates from the day you join. However, there are a few exceptions: Air Canada accepts mileage up to one month prior to enrollment and TWA accepts it up to 10 days. If you have retained your boarding pass/ticket, your mileage may be accepted after flying but before enrolling. It never hurts to try.

Do all flights earn mileage credit?

Most flights do, but there are limits. Limits include: some discount, consolidator or special priced tickets, some economy class tickets on partner airlines, tickets that do not have a fare published on them, bulk fare and charters, and free award travels. If you purchase a ticket, but don't use it, you don't get credit. The good news is that business and first class tickets will often earn you bonus credit.

So should I go with the airline that has the highest minimum per trip credit?

You rack up mileage faster - but check to see how many miles it takes to earn an award. Even though you have more miles with one airline, they may not be worth as much as another airline's.

How do I earn car rental or hotel credit?

By doing business with one of the airline's rental agency or hotel partners. Give them your membership number when making reservations. Some programs stipulate that you must fly on the sponsoring airline to the location of the rental agency or hotel. Other programs let you earn it at any time. Make sure to read your program information brochure.

How do I earn credit for use of a credit card or a specific phone company?

Some of the programs are affiliated with a bank and/or a phone company. Typically, for each dollar spent on the program's credit card, you earn a mile. For each dollar spent through the program's affiliated phone company, you earn between one to five miles.

How do I earn miles for using same or next day delivery?

Some of the airlines offer a cargo delivery service and include it in their frequent flyer bonuses. For example: Arrange to send your 70 pounds or less package on

TWA's "next flight out" small package service and you can receive between 500 miles (for domestic deliveries) and 1,000 miles (for international deliveries) on your frequent flyer program.

How do I keep track of all my miles?

Frequent flyer programs keep count in two ways: One way is to send you periodic statements of credits and or withdrawals. A second tracking method is to send automatic issuance of certificates after a designated amount of miles (which you trade in for awards). *If you move, make sure to notify your program; your statements and awards are not automatically forwarded.

What if my miles don't get credited?

Always keep your original passenger receipt, boarding pass and hotel/car rental agreements. Make copies and send these along with your full name, membership number, dates of travel, class of service and your origin and destination, to the program if credit is not shown within a reasonable amount of time or if there is a discrepancy. It is your responsibility to monitor your account.

If there is a discrepancy and you don't have your ticket and boarding pass, the airline may not credit you. You should always write the airline anyway with an explanation and ask.

How do I claim my awards?

You can receive awards in one of two ways. Either a certificate will be automatically sent to you or you will need to send in a claim form that comes with your periodic mileage summary.

How do I make arrangements to fly with my free ticket?

Tell the reservation clerk you are traveling on an award and give them the number of your certificate. If you don't advise them, you may lose your reservation; there are only a specified number of seats per flight allocated to "award travel." You may use it for prepaid tickets or tickets by mail.

Can I use my free ticket at any time?

Not necessarily. Different airlines have different policies towards "blackouts" and "peak seasons." The quickest way to earn a free trip would be to allow the airline to decide when -- season, day, time -- that you would fly. If you want to take your trip during a peak season, you may need to have/use more mileage credit. Usually, the days right around the major holidays are blacked out. Airlines only set aside so many frequent flyer seats per flight and may not offer them on some flights.

How many award certificates may I use per flight?

One. You cannot combine awards.

Who can use the award?
The individual whose name is on the passenger flight coupon, or in some cases, their traveling companion. Some programs allow you to transfer awards to relatives or friends.

What are some other potential benefits?
You can upgrade free economy trips for a small charge (between $15 -$125). You can also get free companion tickets, upgrades for as low as 10,000 miles and frequent flyer special promotions.

How long is an award good for?
The awards have an expiration date - usually one year after issuance. There are no extensions. Typically, when traveling, your return date must be before the expiration date.

If I don't fly very frequently, does mileage credit expire?
In some programs it does. This is usually after three years of inactivity on your account. Your account is then closed and your number is reassigned.

If I accumulate miles over a period of time, how do they decide which miles to put toward the award first?

The oldest mileage is used first. For some programs it is your responsibility to use the oldest awards first.

What if I don't take my earned trip, but want my mileage re-credited?

Read up on your program, it may cost you $50 to re-credit your miles.

How about retroactive crediting for current members?

If you were a member at the time of travel, many programs will allow you six months to send in for credit.

Are there any downfalls in flying frequent flyer?

If your flight is canceled or delayed, you may not get transferred to another airline. Read the fine print on restricted travel.

What if I buy someone else's ticket or sell/barter mine without the consent of the program?

You would be taking a risk. The ticket may not be honored, it may be confiscated. The traveler would be liable for a full fare cost, any litigation costs and damages. You would be expelled from the program.

Are there any hidden costs?

The awards are subject to income tax, which is the responsibility of the recipient. Departure Taxes from USA maybe collected on international flights - this tax is included in the price of a purchased ticket.

Every program is full of the "R" word **RESTRICTION**. Read the fine print or call a program representative with all your questions.

TAKING ADVANTAGE OF YOUR FREQUENT-FLYER PROGRAM

The bottomline is to keep it simple. We recommend the following:

- Join one or two programs and fly only those airlines. You will accumulate mileage quicker and be able to audit your mileage more efficiently.
- Choose an airline that flies to the destinations you are seeking or whose affiliate/partner airline has routings to.
- Use the products and/or services affiliated or partnered with that airline. ie... hotels, car rentals, long distance phone companies etc.
- Fly during bonus-mile promotions.
- Read the literature mailed to you from your frequent flyer program. These mailings often contain advance information and/or valuable coupons.

AIR CANADA
Aeroplan (800) 361-8253
Partner Airlines
Singapore Airlines
Air France
Voyager Airlines
Finnair
First Air
Austria Airlines
Austrian Air Service
Bearskin Airlines
Cathay Pacific Airlines
Partner Car Rental Agencies
Avis
Budget
Partner Hotels
The Charlottetown
Coast Holiday
Hilton and Hilton International
Hotel Des Gouverneurs
Keddy's
Radisson
Sheraton
Westin
Bonus Packages
Special Promotions
First Class and Business Bonuses
Enrollment Bonus, 4,000 bonus miles if you fly within 45 days of membership.
Minimum Mileage Award
250
Awards Issued
Periodic Statements

ALASKA AIRLINES
Mileage Plan (800) 654-5669
Partner Airlines
British Airways
Era Aviation
Horizon
LAB
Markair
Northwest Airlines
Reeve
SAS
Temsco
Thai
TWA
Partner Car Rental Agencies
Alamo
Budget
National
Partner Hotels
Holiday Inn
Hyatt
Red Lion
West Coast
Westin
Westmark
Credit Card
Seafirst Bank
Phone Company
AlasCom (TAMAM)
Bonus Packages
Vacation Plans
First Class Bonuses
Minimum Miles Awarded 500
Awards Issued Periodic Statements

AMERICA WEST AIRLINES
Flight Fund (800) 247-5691
Partner Airlines
Air France
Virgin Atlantic
Partner Car Rental Agencies
Budget
Hertz
Thrifty
Partner Hotels
Compri
Doubletree
Marriott Hotels and Resorts
Red Lion
Westin
Credit Card
None
Phone Company
None
Bonus Packages
First Class and Business Bonuses
Enrollment Bonus, 2,500 miles
Minimum Miles Awarded
750
Awards Issued
Automatically

AMERICAN AIRLINES
Advantage (800) 882-8880
Partner Airlines
American Eagle
British Airways
Cathay Pacific Airways
Qantas
Reno Air
Singapore
TWA
TWExpress
Partner Car Rental Agencies
Ansa
Avis
Hertz
Partner Hotels
Aston
Forum Hotels
Hilton Hotels and Resorts
Inter Continental Hotels
ITT Sheraton Inns, Resorts, All Suites
Marriott Hotels, Resorts, Suites
Wyndham Hotels and Resorts
Credit Card
Advantage CitiBank Visa or Mastercard
Phone Company
MCI Long Distance
SNET Cellular
Bonus Packages
American Traveler Catalog
First Class and Business Bonuses
Minimum Miles Awarded 500
Awards Issued Periodic Statement

CONTINENTAL AIRLINES
One Pass (713) 952-1630
Partner Airlines
Aer Lingus
Alitalia
Cayman
Continental Express
Iberia
KLM
Lan Chile
SAS
Trump Shuttle
Partner Car Rental Agencies
General
National
Thrifty
Partner Hotels
Aston
Camino Real
Consort
Doubletree
Marriott
Radisson
Credit Card
Marine Midland Bank Mastercard
American Express Membership Miles
Phone Company None
Bonus Packages
Privilege Packages
Seasonal Promotions
Enrollment Bonus, 2,500 miles first flight bonus
Minimum Miles Awarded 500
Awards Issued Periodic Statements

DELTA AIRLINES
Frequent Flyer (800) 323-2323
Partner Airlines
Air Canada
Air New Zealand
Japan Airlines
KLM Royal Dutch Airlines
Lufthansa
Singapore Airlines
Swissair
Partner Car Rental Agencies
Alamo
Avis
National
Partner Hotels
Conrad Hotels
Forte Hotels
Hilton Hotels and Resorts
Hilton International
Hyatt
Marriott Hotels, Resorts and Suites
Credit Card
American Express Membership Miles
Phone Company
None
Bonus Packages
First Class and Business Bonuses
Enrollment bonus, 5,000 miles
Minimum Miles Awarded
1,000
Awards Issued
Periodic Statements

NORTHWEST AIRLINES
World Perks (800) 327-2881
Partner Airlines
Alaska Airlines
KLM Royal Dutch
Partner Car Rental Agencies
Budget
Hertz
National
Partner Hotels
Holiday Inn
Hyatt
Marriott
Radisson
Westin
Credit Card
World Perks Visa
American Express Membership Miles
Phone Company
MCI Long Distance
Bonus Packages
Northwest World Vacations
First Class and Business Bonuses
Minimum Miles Awarded
750
Awards Issued
Periodic Statements-awards issued automatically in the
form of tickets

TRANS WORLD AIRLINES
Frequent Flyer Bonus (800) 325-4815
Partner Airlines
Air India
Air New Zealand
Alaska Airlines
American Airlines
New York Helicopter
Philippine Airlines
TWE
Partner Car Rental Agencies
Dollar
Thrifty
Partner Hotels
Adam's Mark Hotel
Doubletree
Forte
Marriott Hotels, Resorts and Suites Trusthouse
Credit Card
Chase Manhattan TWA Visa
Phone Company
Metro Media Communication Corporation
Bonus Packages
Privilege Package
First Class and Business Bonuses
Enrollment Bonus, 3,000 miles
Minimum Miles Awarded
750
Awards Issued
   Periodic Statements

UNITED AIRLINES
Mileage Plus (800) 421-4655
Partner Airlines
Air France
Alitalia
Aloha Airlines
Aloha Island Air
British Airways
Iberia
KLM Royal Dutch Airlines
Lufthansa
SABENA World Airways
SAS
Swissair
United Express
Partner Car Rental Agencies
Alamo
Dollar
Hertz
National
Partner Hotels
Hilton
Hyatt Hotels and Resorts
Inter-Continental Hotels
ITT Sheraton Hotels
Kempski Hotels
Westin Hotels and Resorts
Credit Card
Mileage Plus First Visa/Mastercard Card/Gold
Bonus Packages
United Airlines Travel Card
First Class and Business Bonuses
Minimum Miles Awarded 500
Awards Issued Automatically

USAIR
Frequent Traveler Program (800) 872-4738
Partner Airlines
Air France
Air New Zealand
Alitalia
All Nippon Airlines
British Airways
KLM Royal Dutch Airlines
Lufthansa
Northwest
SABENA World Airways
Swissair
Partner Car Rental Agencies
Hertz
National
Partner Hotels
Hilton
Hyatt
Marriott
Omni
Radisson
Stouffer
Westin
Credit Card
USAir Visa
Phone Company
None
Bonus Packages
First Class and Business Bonuses
Enrollment Bonus, 2,000 if you travel within 60 days of
membership.
Minimum Miles Awarded 750
Awards Issued Periodic Statements

AIRLINE PHONE DIRECTORY

ALM Antillean Airlines (800) 327-7230
Caribbean

ANA - All Nippon Airways (800) 235-9262
Japan

Aer Lingus (800) 223-6537
Ireland

Aero California (800) 237-6225
Mexico - Baja California

Aerolineas Argentinas (800) 333-0276
Argentina

Aeromexico (800) 237-6639
Mexico

Aeroperu (800) 777-7717
Peru

Air Afrique (800) 456-9192
Africa

Air Canada (800) 776-3000
Canada

Air France (800) 237-2747
France

Air India (800) 223-7776
India

Air Inter (800) 237-2747
France

Air Jamaica (800) 523-5585
Jamaica

Air New Zealand (800) 262-1234
New Zealand

Air Paraguay Airlines (800) 677-7771
Paraguay

Alaska Airlines (800) 426-0333
United States - Alaska/Northwest

ALIA Royal Jordanian Airlines (800) 223-0470
Jordan

Alitalia Airlines (800) 223-5730
Italy

Aloha Airlines (800) 367-5250
United States - Hawaii

Alpha Air (800) 421-9353
Mammoth/Grand Canyon

America West Airlines (800) 247-5692
United States

American Airlines (800) 424-7225
United States, International

Ansett Airlines (800) 366-1300
Australia

Austrian Airlines (800) 843-0002
Austria

Avianca (800) 284-2622
Colombia

Aviateca Airlines (800) 327-9832
Guatemala

Bahamasair (800) 562-7661
Bahamas

British Airways (800) 247-9297
England

BWIA International (800) 538-2942
Caribbean Islands

Canadian Airlines International (800) 426-7000
Canada

Carnival (800) 437-2110

Cathay Pacific Airways Ltd.(800) 233-2742
Hong Kong

Cayman Airways (800) 422-9626
Cayman Islands

China Airlines (800) 227-5118
China

Continental Airlines (800) 435-0040
United States, International

Delta Airlines (800) 221-1212
United States, International

Eagle Air (800) 332-4533

Ecuatoriana Airlines (800) 328-2367
Ecuador

Egypt Air (800) 334-6787
Egypt

El Al Israel Airlines (800) 223-6700
Israel

Ethiopian Airlines (800) 433-9677
Ethiopia

Faucett, The First Airline of Peru (800) 334-3356
Peru

Finnair (800) 950-5000
Finland

Florida Shuttle (800) 359-7688

Garuda Indonesian Airways (800) 342-7832
Indonesia

Hawaiian Airlines (800) 367-5320
United States - Hawaii

Iberia Airlines of Spain (800) 772-4642
Spain

Icelandair(800) 223-5500
Iceland

Japan Airlines (800) 525-3663
Japan

Kenya Airways (800) 343-2506
Kenya

Kiwi (800) 538-5494

KLM Royal Dutch Airlines (800) 374-7747
Netherlands

Korean Air (800) 438-5000
Korea

Kuwait Airways (800) 458-9248
Kuwait

LACSA Airlines (800) 225-2272
Central America

LTU International Airways (800) 888-0200
Germany

Ladeco Airlines (800) 825-2332
Chile

Lan-Chile Airlines (800) 735-5526
Chile

Lot Polish Airlines (800) 223-0593
Poland

Lloyd Aereo Boliviano Airlines (800) 327-7407

Lufthansa German Airlines (800) 645-3880
Germany

MGM Grand Air (800) 275-4646
United States

Malaysia Airlines System (800) 421-8641
Malaysia

Malev Hungarian Airlines (800) 223-6884
Hungary

Mark Air (800) 426-6784
Alaska

Martinair-Holland (800) 366-4655
Holland

Mexicana Airlines (800) 531-7921
Mexico

Midwest Express Airlines (800) 452-2022
United States

Morris Air (800) 466-7747
United States

Mount Cook Airline of New Zealand
New Zealand (800) 468-2665

Northwest Airlines (800) 225-2525
United States/ International (800) 447-4747

Olympic Airways (800) 223-1226
Greece

Pakistan International Airlines (800) 221-2552
Pakistan

Philippine Airlines (800) 435-9725
Philippines

Private Jet (800) 949-9400
United States

Qantas Airways (800) 227-4500
Australia

Reeve Aleutian Airways (800) 544-2248
Alaska

Reno Air (800) 736-6247
Western United States

Royal Air Moroc (800) 344-6726
Morocco

Royal Nepal Airlines (800) 922-7622
Nepal

Sahsa Honduras Airlines (800) 327-1225
Honduras

Sabena World Airways (800) 955-2000
Belgium

Saudi Arabian Airlines (800) 472-8342
Saudi Arabia

Scandinavian Airlines - SAS (800) 221-2350
Scandinavia

Singapore Airlines (800) 742-3333
Singapore

Sky Shuttle (800) 735-6743

Skywest Airlines (800) 453-9417
Australia

South African Airways (800) 722-9675
South Africa

Southwest Airlines (800) 435-9792
United States - South, West, Midwest

Spirit Airlines (800) 435-9792
United States

Surinam Airways (800)327-6864
Surinam

Swissair (800) 221-4750
Switzerland

TACA International Airlines (800) 535-8780
El Salvador

TAP Air Portugal (800) 221-7370
Portugal

Thai Airways International (800) 426-5204
Thailand

Tower Air (800) 348-6937

Trans-Brazil (800) 872-3153
Brazil

TWA-Trans World Airways (800) 221-2000
United States/ International

USAir (800) 428-4322
United States

United Airlines (800) 537-7783
United States/ International

UTA-French Airlines (800) 237-2747
France, Polynesia

Varig Brasilian Airlines (800) 468-2744
Brasil

Viasa Venezuelan Int'l Airways (800) 468-4272
Venezuela

Virgin Atlantic Airways (800) 862-8621
England

Wings of the World (800) 835-9969

Yemen Airways (800) 257-1133
Yemen

FOREIGN ENTRY REQUIREMENTS

visa, passport, immunizations and embassy contacts

The bulk of following information was written by the United States Department of State - Bureau of Consular Affairs prior to February 1993. This information is subject to change, and as such, we recommend checking with the consular officials of the country(s) to be visited well in advance of departure.

AFGHANISTAN - Passport and visa required. No tourist or business visas are being are being issued at this time. For further information, contact Embassy of the Republic of Afghanistan, 2341 Wyoming Ave., N.W., Washington, D.C. 20008 (202/234-3770-1).

ALBANIA - Passport and visa required. For further information contact the Embassy of Albania at 1150 18th Street NW, Washington, D.C., 20036 (202/223-4942).

ALGERIA - Passport and visa required. Obtain visa before arrival. Visa valid up to 90 days, requires 2 application forms, 2 photos, proof of onward/return transportation, sufficient funds and $22 fee (money order or certified check). Company letter (+ 1 copy) required for business visa. Visas not granted to passports showing Israeli visas. Enclose prepaid self-addressed envelope for return of passport by registered, certified or Express Mail. For currency regulations and other information, contact the consular section of the Embassy of the Democratic and Popular Republic of Algeria, 2137 Wyoming Ave., NW, Washington, D.C. 20008 (202/263-2800).

ANDORRA - (See France.)

ANGOLA - Passport and visa required. There is no U.S. representation in Angola at this time. Travel by U.S. citizens is not recommended. For additional information, contact the Angolan Permanent Representative to the U.N., 747 3rd Avenue, 18th Floor, New York, N.Y. 10017.

ANTIGUA AND BARBUDA - Proof of U.S. citizenship required, return/onward ticket and/or proof of funds needed for tourist stay up to 6 months. Check Embassy of Antigua and Barbuda, Intelsat Bldg., Suite 4M, 3400 International Drive, N.W., Washington, D.C., 20008 (202/362-5122/5166/5211) for further information.

ARGENTINA - Passport required. Visa is not required for tourist stay up to 3 months. Business visa requires company letter detailing purpose of trip and length of stay. For official and other types of travel information, contact Argentine Embassy, 1600 New Hampshire Ave., N.W., Washington, D.C. 20009 (202/939-6400) or the nearest Consulate: CA (213/739-5959 and 415/982-3050), FL (305.373-1889), IL (312/263-7435), LA (504/523-2823), NY (212/603-0415), PR (809/754-6500) or TX (713/871-8935).

ARMENIA - Passport and visa required. For additional information, contact the consular section of the Embassy of Armenia, 122 C Street, N.W., Suite 360, Washington, D.C., 20001 (202/393-5983).

ARUBA - Passport or proof of U.S. citizenship required. Visa not required for stay up to 14 days, extendable to 90 days after arrival. Proof of onward/return ticket or sufficient funds for stay may be required. Departure tax $9.50. For further information, consult Embassy of the Netherlands (202/244-5300), or nearest Consulate General: CA (213/380-3440), IL (314/856-1429), NY (212/246-1429) or TX (713/622-8000).

AUSTRALIA - Passport, visa and onward/return transportation required. Transit visa not necessary for up to 8-hour stay at airport. Visitor visa valid 1 year for multiple entries up to 3 months, no charge, requires 1 application and 1 photo. applications for a stay of longer than 3 months or with a validity longer than 1 year, require fee of $25 (U.S.) Need company letter for business visa. Departure tax, $20 (Australian), paid at airport. Minors not accompanied by parent require notarized written parental consent form both parents. AIDS test required for permanent resident visa applicants age 15 and over; U.S. test accepted. Send prepaid envelope for return of passport by mail. Allow 3 weeks for processing. For further information contact the Embassy of Australia, 1601 Mass. Ave., N.W., Washington, D.C. 20036 (800/242-2878,202/797-3000) or the nearest Consulate General: CA (310/469-4300 or 415/362-6160), HI (808/524-5050), IL (312/645-9440), NY (212/245-4000) or TX (713/629-9131).

AUSTRIA - Passport required. Visa not required for stay up to 3 months. For longer stays check, with Embassy of Austria, 3524 International Court, N.W., Washington, D.C. 20008 (202/895-6767) or nearest Consulate General: Los Angeles (310/444-9310), Chicago (312/222-1515) or New York (212/737-6400).

AZERBAIJAN - Passport and visa required. For additional information contact Consular Section of the Embassy of Russia, 1825 Phelps Pl., N.W., Washington, D.C. 20008 (202/939-8916) or the Consulate General in San Francisco (415/202-9800).

AZORES - (See Portugal.)

BAHAMAS - Proof of U.S. citizenship, photo ID and onward/return ticket required for stay up to 8 months.

Passport and residence/work permit needed for residence and business. Permit required for firearms and to import pets. Departure tax of $3 payable at airport. For further information call Embassy of the Commonwealth of the Bahamas, 2220 Massachusetts Ave., N.W., Washington, D.C. 20008 (202/319-2660) or nearest Consulate: Miami (305/373-6295) or New York (212/421-6420).

BAHRAIN - Passport and visa required. No tourist visas issued at this time. Transit visa available upon arrival for stay up to 72 hours, must have return/onward ticket. Business, work, or resident visas valid for 3 months, single-entry, require 1 application form, 1 photo, letter from company or No Objection Certificate (NOC) from Immigration Dept. in Bahrain and $30 fee ($20 for bearer of NOC). Yellow fever vaccination needed if arriving from infected area. Send SASE for return of passport by mail. Holders of passports bearing Israeli stamps will be delayed or denied entry. For departure tax and other information, contact Embassy of the State of Bahrain, 3502 International Drive, N.W., Washington, D.C. 20008 (202/342-0741); or the Permanent Mission to the U.N., 2 United Nations Plaza, East 44th Street, New York, N.Y. 10017

BANGLADESH - Passport, visa and onward/return ticket required. Tourist and business visa requires 2 application forms, 2 photos and company letter. Business visa requires company letter. For longer stays and more information, consult the Embassy of the People's Republic of Bangladesh, 2201 Wisconsin Ave., N.W., Washington, D.C. 20007 (202/342-8373).

BARBADOS - U.S. citizens traveling directly from the

U.S. to Barbados may enter for up to 3 months stay with proof of U.S. citizenship, photo ID and onward/return ticket. Passport required for longer visits and other types of travel. Business visas $25, single-entry and $30 multiple-entry (may require work permit). Departure tax of $25 is paid at airport. Check information with Embassy of Barbados, 2144 Wyoming Ave., N.W., Washington, D.C. 20008 (202/939-9200) or Consulate General in New York (212/867-8435).

BELARUS - Passport and visa required. Visa requires 1 application form and 1 photo. The visa processing fee is $30 for 7 working days, $60 for next day and $100 for same day processing. Transit visa is required when traveling through Belarus ($20). For additional information contact Embassy of Belarus, Suite 619, 1511 K Street, NW., Washington, D.C., 20005-1403 (202/638-2954).

BELGIUM - Passport required. Visa not required for business/tourist stay up to 90 days. Temporary residence permit required for longer stays. For residence authorization, consult Embassy of Belgium, 3330 Garfield St., N.W., Washington, D.C. 20008 (202/333-6900) or nearest Consulate General: Los Angeles (213/857-1244), Atlanta (404/659-2150), Chicago (312/263-6624) or New York (212/586-5110).

BELIZE - Passport, return/onward ticket and sufficient funds required. Visa not required for stay up to 1 month. If visit exceeds 1 month, a stay permit must be obtained from the Immigration Authorities in Belize. AIDS test required for those staying more than 3 months; U.S. test accepted if within 3 months of visit. For longer stays and other information, contact Embassy of Belize, 2535

Massachussetts Ave., N.W., Washington, D.C.   20008 (202/332-9636) or the Belize Mission in New York at (212/599-0233).

BENIN - Passport and visa required. Entry/transit visa for stay up to 90 days, requires $20 fee (no personal checks), 2 application forms, 2 photos, vaccination certificates for yellow fever and cholera, proof of return/onward transportation (guarantee from travel agency or photocopy of round trip ticket) and letter of guarantee from employer. Send prepaid envelope for return of passport by certified or express mail. Apply at Embassy of the Republic of Benin, 2737 Cathedral Ave., N.W., Washington, D.C. 20008 (202/232-6656).

BERMUDA - Proof of U.S. citizenship, photo ID and onward/return ticket required for tourist stay up to 21 days. Departure tax $10 is paid at airport. For further information, consult British Embassy (202/462-1340).

BHUTAN - Passport and visa required. Visa requires $20 fee, 2 applications and 2 photos. Tourist visas arranged by Tourism Department and issued at entry checkpoints in Bhutan. Apply 2 months in advance. For further information call the Consulate of the Kingdom of Bhutan in New York (212/826-1919) or the Bhutan Travel Service, 120 East 56 Street, N.Y., N.Y., (212/838-6382) or the Bhutan travel service, 120 East 56 Street, New York, N.Y. (212/ 838-6382)

BOLIVIA - Passport required. Visa not required for tourist stay up to 30 days. Business visa requires $50 fee, company letter with purpose of trip one photo and one application form. Send SASE for return of passport by mail. For official/diplomatic travel contact Embassy of Bolivia (Consular Section), 3014 Mass. Ave., N.W., Washington, D.C. 20008 (202/232-4828 or 483-4410) or nearest Consulate General: San Francisco (415/495-5173), Miami (305/358-3450), New York (212/687-0530) or Houston (713/780-8001). Check requirements for pets.

BOSNIA AND HERZEGOVINA - Passport required. At the time of publication, Bosnia-Herzegovina entry permission is being granted at the border on a case by-case basis.

BOTSWANA - Passport required. Visa not required for stay up to 90 days. For further information, contact Embassy of the Republic of Botswana, Suite 7M, 3400 International Drive, N.W., Washington, D.C. 20008 (202/244-4990/1) or nearest Honorary Consulate: Los Angeles (213/626-8484), San Francisco (415/346-4435) or Houston (713/622-1900).

BRAZIL - Passport and visa required. Visa must be obtained in advance. Multiple-entry visa valid up to 90 days (extendable), requires 1 application form, 1 photo, proof of onward/return transportation or notarized letter from bank as proof of sufficient funds for stay and yellow fever vaccination if arriving from infected area. No charge if you apply in person, $10 service fee if you apply by mail. Provide SASE for return of passport by mail. For travel with children or business visa contact Brazilian Embassy (Consular Section) 3009 Whitehaven St., N.W., Washington, D.C. 20008 (202/745-2828) or nearest Consulate: CA (213/651-2664), FL (305/285-6200), IL (312/372-2177), LA (504/588-9187) or NY (212/464-0244).

BRUNEI - Passport and visa required. Visa must be obtained in advance. Visa valid 3 months requires $7.50 fee, 1 application form, 2 photos, letter stating purpose of visit, itinerary, onward/return ticket and proof of sufficient funds. Yellow fever vaccination needed if arriving from infected area. Include prepaid envelope for return of passport by certified/registered mail. Allow at least 1 week for processing. For diplomatic/official travel and other visas, contact Embassy of the State of Brunei Darussalam, Suite 300, 2600 Virginia Ave., N.W., Washington, D.C. 20037 (202/342-0159) or Brunei Permanent Mission to the U.N., 866 United Nations Plaza, Rm. 248, New York, N.Y., 10017 (212/838-1600).

BULGARIA- Passport required. Tourist visa not required for stay up to 30 days. AIDS test required for those staying more than 1 month; U.S. test not accepted. For business visas and other information contact Embassy of the Republic of Bulgaria, 1621 22nd St., N.W., Washington, D.C. 20008 (202/387-7969 or 483-5885).

BURKINA FASO - Passport and visa required. Single-entry visa valid 3 months for visit up to 1 month, extendable, requires $20 fee, 2 application forms, 2 photos and yellow fever vaccination (cholera immunization recommended). Send passport by registered mail and include postage or prepaid envelope for return. Cash or money order only. For further information call Embassy of Burkina Faso, 2340 Mass. Ave., N.W., Washington, D.C. 20008 (202/332-5577) or Honorary Consulate in Decatur, GA (404/378-7278), Los Angeles, CA (213/824-5100) or New Orleans, LA (504/945-3152).

BURMA - (See Myanmar.)

BURUNDI - Passport and visa required. Obtain visa before arrival to avoid long airport delay. Multi-entry visa valid for 2 months (must be used within 2 months of date of issue) requires $11 fee, 3 application forms, 3 photos, yellow fever and cholera immunizations and return/onward ticket. Meningitis immunization recommended. Company letter needed for business travel. Send U.S. postal money order only and SASE for return of passport by mail. For further information consult Embassy of the Republic of Burundi, Suite 212, 2233 Wisconsin Ave., N.W., Washington, D.C. 20007 (202/342-2574) or Permanent Mission of Burundi to the U.N. (212/687-1180).

CAMBODIA - (formerly Kampuchea) Passport and visa required. There is no Cambodian Embassy in the U.S. at this time. Visas must be obtained from a Cambodian Embassy or Consulate in a country which maintains diplomatic relations with Cambodia.

CAMEROON -

CANADA - Proof of U.S. citizenship and photo ID required. Visa not required for tourists entering from the U.S. for a stay up to 180 days. However, a Minister's Permit is required for anyone with a criminal record (including a DWI charge). U.S. citizens entering Canada from a third country must have a valid passport or official U.S. travel document. For student or business travel, check with the Canadian Embassy, 501 Pennsylvania Ave., N.W., Washington, D.C. 20001 (202/682-1740) or nearest Consulate General: CA (213/687-7432 and 415/495-6021), GA (404/577-6810), IL (312/427-

1031), MA (617/262-3760), MI (313/567-2340), MN (612/333-4641), NY (212/768-2400), OH (216/771-0150), TX (214/922-9806) or WA (206/443-1777).

CAPE VERDE - Passport and visa required. Single-entry tourist visa (must be used within 120 days of issue), requires $13 fee, 1 application form, 1 photo and yellow fever immunization if arriving from infected area. Include SASE for return of passport by mail. For further information contact the Embassy of the Republic of Cape Verde, 3415 Mass., Ave., N.W., Washington, D.C. 20007 (202/965-6820) or Consulate General: 535 Boylston St., Boston, MA 02116 (617/353-0014).

CAYMAN ISLANDS - (See West Indies, British.)

CENTRAL AFRICAN REPUBLIC - Passport and visa required. Visa must be obtained before arrival. To obtain a visa you need 2 application forms, 2 recent photos, yellow fever immunization, onward/return ticket and SASE for return of passport by mail and $30 fee. Company letter needed for business visa. For further information contact Embassy of Central African Republic, 1618 22nd St., N.W., Washington, D.C. 20008 (202/483-7800/1).

CHAD - Passport and visa required. Transit visa valid for up to 1 week and requires onward ticket. Single-entry visa valid 2 months for tourist/business stay up to 30 days (extendable), requires $25 fee, yellow fever and cholera vaccinations, 3 application forms and 3 photos. For business visa, you need company letter stating purpose of trip. Send prepaid envelope for registered/certified return of passport. Apply Embassy for the

Republic of Chad, 2002 R St., N.W., Washington, D.C. 20009 (202/462-4009), and check specific requirements.

CHILE - Passport required. Visa not required for stay up to 3 months, may be extended. For official/diplomatic travel and other information consult Embassy of Chile, 1732 Mass Ave., N.W., Washington, D.C. 20036 (202/785-3159) or nearest Consulate General: CA (213/624-6357 and 415/982-7662), FL (305/373-8623), PA (215/829-9520), NY (212/980-3366) or TX (713/621-5853) or PR (809/725-6365).

CHINA, PEOPLE'S REPUBLIC OF - Passport and visa required. Transit visa required for any stop (even if you do not exit the plane or train) in China. Visitors must show hotel reservation and "letter of confirmation" from the China International Travel Service (CITS) or an invitation from an individual or institution in China. CITS tours may be booked through several travel agencies and airlines in the United States and abroad, often advertised in newspapers and magazines. Visas for tour group members are usually obtained by the travel agent as part of the tour package. Visa requires $10 fee, 2 application forms and 2 photos. Allow at least 10 days processing time. Medical examination required for those staying 1 year or longer. AIDS test required for those staying more than 6 months. For further information contact Chinese Embassy, 2300 Connecticut Ave., N.W., Washington, D.C. 20008 (202/328-2517) or nearest Consulate General: Chicago (312/346-0287), Houston (713/524-0780), Los Angeles (213/380-2508), New York (212/279-4275) or San Francisco (415/563-4885).

COLOMBIA - Passport and proof of onward/return ticket and entry permit required for stay up to 90 days. Entry permits issued at port of entry. For information about longer stays, business and official travel contact Embassy of Colombia (Consulate), 1825 Conn. Ave., N.W., Washington, D.C. 20009 (202/332-7476) or nearest Consulate General: CA (213/362-1137), FL (305.448-5558), GA (404/237-1045) IL (312/341-0658), LA (504/525-5580), MA (617/536-6222), MI (313/352-4970), MN (612/933-2408), MO (314/991-3636), OH (216/943-1200), NY (212/949-9898), PR (809/754-6885) or TX (713/527-8919).

COMOROS ISLANDS - Passport and onward/return ticket. Visa for up to 3 weeks (extendable) issued at airport upon arrival. For further information consult Embassy of the Federal and Islamic Republic of Comoros, 336 East 45th St., 2nd Floor, New York, NY 10017 (212/972-8010).

CONGO - Passport and visa required. Single-entry visa or multiple-entry $25, for tourist/business stay up to 3 months, requires yellow fever and cholera immunizations and onward/return ticket. First-time applicants need 3 application forms and 3 photos, returning visitors need only 2. For business visa, you must have company letter stating reason for trip. Include SASE for return passport by mail. Letter of introduction stating reason for trip, 3 applications and 3 photos required. Apply Embassy of the People's Republic of the Congo, 4891 Colorado Ave., N.W., Washington, D.C., 20011 (202/726-5500/1).

COOK ISLANDS - Passport and onward/return ticket required. Visa not needed for visit up to 31 days. For longer stays and further information contact Consulate for the Cook Islands, Kamehameha Schools, #16,

Kapalama Heights, Honolulu, HI 96817 (808/847-6377).

COSTA RICA - Valid passport required. Travelers are sometimes admitted with (original) certified U.S. birth certificate and photo ID for tourist stay up to 90 days. Tourist card issued upon arrival at airport. U.S. citizens must have onward/return ticket. For stays over 90 days, you must apply for an extension (within first week of visit) with Costa Rican Immigration and, after 90 days, obtain exit visa and possess a valid U.S. passport. Visitors staying over 90 days must have an AIDS test performed in Costa Rica. For travel with pets and other information contact Embassy of Costa Rica, 1825 Conn. Ave., N.W., Suite 211, Washington, D.C. 20009 (202/328-6628) or nearest Consulate General: CA (415/392-8488), FL (305/377-4242), IL (312/263-2772), LA (504/525-5445), NY (212/425-2620) or TX (713/785-1315).

COTE D'IVOIRE (formerly Ivory Coast) - Passport required. Visa not required for stay up to 90 days. Visa $33, requires 4 application forms, 4 photos, yellow fever vaccination, onward/return ticket and financial guarantee. Include postage for return of passport by registered mail. For further information contact Embassy of the Republic of Cote D'Ivoire, 2424 Mass. Ave., N.W., Washington, D.C. 20008 (202/797-0300) or Honorary Consulate: CA (415/391-0176).

CROATIA- Embassy of Croatia (202/543-5580 or 5608).

CUBA - Passport and visa required. Tourist visa $26, business visa $36, valid up to 6 months, requires 1 application and photo. Send money order only and SASE for return of passport. Apply Cuban Interests

Section, 2639 16th Street, N.W., Washington, D.C. 20009 (202/797-8609 or 8518). AIDS test required for those staying longer than 90 days. **Attention:** U.S. citizens need a Treasury Dept. license in order to engage in any transaction related to travel to and within Cuba. Before planning any travel to Cuba, U.S. citizens should contact the Licensing Division, Office of Foreign Assets Control, Department of the Treasury, 1331 G St., N.W., Washington, D.C. 20220 (202/622-2480).

CURACAO - (See Netherlands Antilles).

CYPRUS - Passport required. Tourist/business visa issued on arrival for stay up to 3 months. Departure tax of $8 paid at airport. AIDS test required for certain entertainers; U.S. test accepted. For other information, consult Embassy of the Republic of Cyprus, 2211 R St., N.W., Washington, D.C. 20008 (202/462-5772) or nearest Consulate: San Francisco (415/893-1661), Chicago (312/677-9068), St. Louis (314/781-7040) or New York (212/686-6016).

CZECH REPUBLIC - Passport required. Visa not required for stay up to 30 days. For longer stays and other types of travel contact Embassy of Czech Republic, 3900 Spring of Freedom Street, N.W., Washington, D.C. 20008 (202/363-6315).

DENMARK (including **GREENLAND**) - Passport required. Tourist/business visa not required for stay up to 3 months. (Period begins when entering Scandinavian area: Finland, Iceland, Norway, Sweden.) Special rules apply for entry into the U.S. - operated defense area in Greenland. For further information, contact the Royal

Danish Embassy, 3200 Whitehaven St., N.W., Washington, D.C. 20008 (202/234-4300) or nearest Consulate General: CA (213/387-4277), Chicago (312/329-9644) or New York (212/223-4545).

DJIBOUTI - Passport and visa required. Visas must be obtained before arrival. Single-entry visa valid for 30 days, extendable, requires $15 fee, 2 applications, 2 photos, yellow fever immunization, onward/return ticket and sufficient funds. Company letter needed for business visa. Send prepaid envelope for return of passport by registered, certified, or express mail. Apply Embassy of the Republic of Djibouti, 1156 15th St., N.W., Suite 515, Washington, D.C. 20005 (202/331-0270) or the Djibouti Mission to the U.N., 866 United Nations Plaza, Suite 4011, New York, N.Y. 10017 (212/753-3163).

DOMINICA - Proof of U.S. citizenship, photo ID and return/onward ticket required for tourist stay up to 6 months. For longer stays and other information, consult Consulate of the Commonwealth of Dominica, 820 2nd Ave., Suite 900, New York, N.Y. 10017 (212/599-8478).

DOMINICAN REPUBLIC - Passport or proof of U.S. citizenship and tourist card or visa required. Tourist card for stay up to 60 days, available from Consulate or from airline serving the country, $10 fee. Visa issued by Consulate, valid up to 5 years, no charge. All persons must pay $10 airport fee. For business travel and other information call the Embassy of the Dominican Republic, 1715 22nd St., N.W., Washington, D.C. 20008 (202/332-6280) or nearest Consulate General: CA (213/858-7365), FL (305/358-3221), IL (312/772-6362), LA (504-522-1843), MA (617/482-8121), NY (212/768-2480), PA (215/923-3006) or PR (809/725-9550).

ECUADOR - Passport and return/onward ticket required for stay up to 3 months. For additional information, contact the Embassy of Ecuador, 2535 15th St., N.W., Washington, D.C. 20009 (202/234-7166) or nearest Consulate General: CA (213/628-3014 or 415/391-4148), FL (305/539-8214), IL (312/642-8579), LA (504/523-3229), MA (617/227-7200), NY (212/683-7555) or TX (214/747-6329).

EGYPT - Passport and visa required. Travel not advised at this time. For additional information, consult the Embassy of the Arab Republic of Egypt, 2310 Decatur Pl., NW Washington, D.C. 20008 (202/234-3903)

EL SALVADOR - Passport and visa required. Visa valid up to 90 days, requires $10 fee, 1 application form and 1 photo and letter stating purpose/length of trip. Personal checks not accepted. Length of stay determined by immigration authorities upon arrival. Allow 10 days for processing. Send SASE for return of passport by mail. Apply Consulate General of El Salvador, 1010 16th Street, N.W., 3rd floor, Washington, D.C. 20036 (202/331-4032) or nearest Consulate: CA (213/383-5776 or 415/781-7924), FL (305/371-8850), LA (504/522-4266), NY (212/889-3608) or TX (713/270-6239).

ENGLAND - (See United Kingdom.)

EQUATORIAL GUINEA - Passport and visa required. Obtain visa in advance. For further information, contact the residence of the Ambassador of Equatorial Guinea at 57 Magnolia Ave., Mount Vernon, N.Y. (914/667-9664)

ESTONIA - Passport and visa required. Visas for entry or transit are issued at the Estonia border at time of entry (no charge). For further information, check Embassy of the Republic of Estonia, 9 Rockefeller Plaza, Suite J-1421, New York, NY 10020 (212/247-1450).

ERITREA - Passport and travel permit required. Travel permit may be obtained from the Washington office of the Provisional Government of Eritrea, 1418 15th Street, Suite 1, P.O. Box 65685, Washington, D.C. 20035 (202/265-3070).

ETHIOPIA - Passport and visa required. Tourist/business visa valid for stay up to 30 days, fee $20 or transit visa for 48 hours, requires 1 application, 1 photo and yellow fever immunization. Business visa requires company letter and approval from Foreign Ministry in Addis Ababa (allow extra time for processing). Send $2 postage for return of passport of $15 for express mail service. Personal checks not accepted and allow two weeks for processing. Exit visas are required of all visitors staying longer than 30 days. For longer stays and other information, contact Embassy of Ethiopia, 2134 Kalorama Rd., N.W., Washington, D.C. 20008 (202/234-2281/2).

FIJI - Passport, proof of sufficient funds and onward/return ticket required. Visa issued on arrival for stay up to 30 days and may be extended up to 6 months. For further information, contact Embassy of Fiji, 2233 Wisconsin Ave., N.W., #240, Washington, D.C. 20007 (202/337-8320) or Mission to the U.N., One United Nations Plaza, 26th Floor, New York, N.Y. 10017 (212/355-6007).

FINLAND - Passport required. Tourist/business visa not required for stay up to 90 days. 90 day period begins when entering Scandinavian area: Sweden, Norway, Denmark, Iceland.) Check Embassy of Finland, 3216 New Mexico Ave., N.W., Washington, D.C. 20016 (202/363-2430) or nearest Consulate General: Los Angeles (213/203-9903) or New York (212/573-6007)

FRANCE - Passport required to visit France, Andorra, Monaco, Corsica and French Polynesia. Visa not required for tourist/business stay up to 3 months in France, Andorra, Monaco and Corsica, and 1 month in French Polynesia. For further information, consult Embassy of France, 4101 Reservoir Rd., N.W., Washington, D.C. 20007 (202/944-6200/6215) or nearest Consulate: CA (310/479-4426 or 415/397-4330), FL (305/372-9798), GA (404/522-4226) HI (808/599-4458), IL (312/787-5359), LA (504/523-5774), ME (617/482-3650), MI (313/568-0990), NY (212/606-3688), PR (809/753-1700) or TX (713/528-2183).

FRENCH GUIANA - Proof of U.S. citizenship and photo ID required for visit up to 3 weeks. For stays longer than 3 weeks, a passport is required. No visa required for stays up to 3 months. For further information, consult Embassy of France, 4101 Reservoir Rd, NW., Washington, D.C. 20007 (202/944-6200).

FRENCH POLYNESIA - Includes Society Islands, French Southern and Antarctic Lands, Tuamotu, Gambier, French Austral, Marquesas, Kerguelen, Crozet, New Caledonia, Tahiti, Wallis and Furtuna Islands. Passport required. Visa not required for visit up to 1 month. For longer stays and further information, consult Embassy of France (202/944-6200).

GABON - Passport and visa required. Visa applicants must obtain visa before arrival. Single-entry visa valid up to 1 month, requires 2 application forms, 2 photos, yellow fever vaccination and $20 fee. Multiple-entry visa valid for 2-4 months, $50 (no personal checks accepted). Also need detailed travel arrangements, including flight numbers, arrival and departure dates, accommodations and next destination. Business visa requires company letter stating purpose of trip and contacts in Gabon. Accompanying family must be included in letter. For longer stays and other information, call Embassy of the Gabonese Republic, 2034 20th St., N.W., Washington, D.C. 20009 (202/797-1000).

GALAPAGOS ISLANDS - Passport and onward/return ticket required for visits up to 3 months. For further information, consult Embassy of Ecuador (202/234-7166).

GAMBIA - Passport and visa required. Single-entry visa for stay up to 3 months, requires $12 fee, 1 application, 1 photo and yellow fever immunization certificates. Multi-entry visa available, $24. For business visa, need company letter stating purpose of visit and itinerary. Allow at least 2 working days for processing. Include prepaid envelope for return of passport by mail. Apply Embassy of the Gambia, Suite 720, 1030 15th St., N.W., Washington, D.C. 20005 (202/785-1399) or Permanent Mission of The Gambia to the U.N., 820 2nd Ave., 9th Floor, New York, N.Y. 10017 (212/949-6640).

GEORGIA - Passport and visa required. For additional information contact the Consular Section of the Embassy of Russia, 1825 Phelps Pl., N.W., Washington, D.C. 20008

(202/939-8907, 8911 or 8913) or the Consulate General: San Francisco (415/202-9800).

GERMANY - Passport required. Tourist/business visa not required for stay up to 3 months. For longer stays, obtain temporary residence permit upon arrival. AIDS test required of applicants for Bavaria residence permits staying over 180 days; U.S. test not accepted. Every foreigner entering Germany must provide proof of sufficient health insurance. For further information, contact Embassy of the FRG, 4645 Reservoir Rd., N.W., Washington, D.C. 20007 (202/298-4000) or nearest Consulate General: CA (415/775-1061), FL (305/358-0290), MI (313/962-6562), NY (212/308-8700) or TX (713/627-7770).

GHANA - Passport and visa required. Tourist visa required for stay up to 30 days (extendable). Requires $30 fee, 1 application form, 4 photos, copy of onward/return ticket, financial guarantee, yellow fever and cholera immunizations. Allow 3 working days for processing. Include prepaid envelope for return of passport by certified mail. All foreign visitors who remain in Ghana for more than 7 days must register with the Ghana Immigration Service within 48 hours of arrival. For additional information, contact Embassy of Ghana, 3512 International Drive, N.W., Washington, D.C. 20008 (202/686-4520) or Consulate General, 19 East 47th St., New York, N.Y. 10017 (212/832-1300).

GIBRALTAR - Passport required. Visa not required for tourist stay up to 3 months. For further information, consult British Embassy (202/462-1340).

GILBERT ISLANDS - (See Kiribati.)

GREAT BRITAIN AND NORTHERN IRELAND - (See United Kingdom.)

GREECE - Passport required. Visa not required for tourist/business stay up to 3 months. If traveling on diplomatic/official passport, visa required and must be obtained in advance. AIDS test required for performing artists and students on Greek scholarships; U.S. test not accepted. For additional information, consult Consular Section of the Embassy of Greece, 2221 Mass. Ave., N.W., Washington, D.C.   20008 (202/232-8222) or nearest Consulate: CA (415/775-2102), GA (404/261-3313), IL (312/372-5356), LA (504/523-1167), MA (617/542-3240) or NY (212/998-5500).

GREENLAND - (See Denmark.)

GRENADA - Passport is recommended, but tourists may enter with birth certificate and photo ID.   Visa not required for tourist stay up to 3 months, may be extended to maximum of 6 months.   For additional information, consult Embassy of Grenada, 1701 New Hampshire Ave., N.W., Washington, D.C.   20009 (202/265-2561) or Permanent Mission of Grenada to the U.N. (212/687-9554).

GUADELOUPE - (see West Indies, French).

GUATEMALA - Passport and visa, or tourist card required. Tourist card issued by Consulate or airline for $5, valid 30 days for single-entry, requires proof of U.S. citizenship and photo ID. Visas available from Consulate, no charge, valid 1 year, multiple entries of 30 days each, requires passport, 1 application form and 1 photo. Provide SASE for return of passport by mail. Length of stay for the visa and tourist card is determined by immigration authorities upon arrival. For travel by minors and other information, contact Embassy of Guatemala, 2220 R St., N.W., Washington, D.C. 20008 (202/745-4952/4) or nearest Consulate: CA (213/365-9251 or 415/788-5651), FL (305/443-4828/29), NY (212/686-3837) or TX (713/953-9531), IL (312/332-1587).

GUIANA, FRENCH - (See French Guiana.)

GUINEA - Passport and visa required. Tourist/business visa for stay up to 3 months, requires 3 application forms, 3 photos, yellow fever immunization and $25 fee (cash or money order only). Malaria suppressants are recommended. Departure tax $10 ($7 if traveling to another African country) payable at airport. For business visa need company letter stating purpose of trip and letter of invitation from company in Guinea. Provide SASE for return of passport by mail. Apply Embassy of the Republic of Guinea, 2112 Leroy Pl., N.W., Washington, D.C. 20008 (202/483-9420).

GUINEA-BISSAU - Passport and visa required. Visa must be obtained in advance. Visa valid up to 90 days, requires 2 application forms, 2 photos, yellow fever immunization, financial guarantee for the stay and $12 fee payable by money order only. Include prepaid envelope for return of passport by express mail. Apply Embassy of Guinea-Bissau, 918 16th St., N.W., Mezzanine Suite, Washington, D.C. 20006 (202/872-4222).

GUYANA - Passport and visa not required. Single-entry tourist/business visa for stay up to 3 months, no charge, requires 3 application forms and 3 photos. Business visa requires letter from company acknowledging responsibility and purpose of trip. For longer stays, multiple-entry visas and other information, consult Embassy of Guyana, 2490 Tracy Pl., N.W., Washington, D.C. 20008 (202/265-6900/03) or Consulate General, 866 U.N. Plaza, 3rd Floor, New York, NY 10017 (212/527-3215/6).

HAITI - Passport required. For further information, consult Embassy of Haiti, 2311 Mass. Ave., N.W., Washington, D.C. 20008 (202/332-4090/2) or nearest consulate: FL (305/859-2003), MA (617/723-5211), NY (212/697-9767) or PR (809/766-0758).

HOLY SEE, APOSTOLIC NUNCIATURE OF THE - Passport required. Visa not required for tourist stay up to 3 months. For further information, consult Apostolic Nunciature of the Holy See, 3339 Mass. Ave., N.W., Washington, D.C. 20008 (202/333-7121) or call Embassy of Italy (202/328-5500).

HONDURAS - Passport and onward/return ticket required. For additional information, contact Embassy of Honduras (Consular Section), Suite 927, 1511 K Street, N.W., Washington, D.C. 20005 (202/223-0185), or nearest Consulate: CA (213/383-9244 or 415/392-0076), FL (305/447-8927), IL (312/772-7090), LA (504/522-3118), NY (212/269-3611) or TX (713/622-4572).

HONG KONG - Passport and onward/return transportation by sea/air required. Visa not required for tourist stay up to 30 days, may be extended to 3 months. Confirmed hotel and flight reservations recommended during peak travel months. Departure tax 150 Hong Kong Dollars (approx. $20 U.S.) paid at airport. Visa required for work or study, For other types of travel, consult British Embassy (202/462-1340).

HUNGARY - Passport required. Visa not required for stay up to 90 days. For business travel and other information, check Embassy of the Republic of Hungary, 3910 Shoemaker Street, N.W., Washington, D.C. 20008 (202/362-6730) or Consulate General, 8 East 75th Street, New York, N.Y. 10021 (212/879-4127).

ICELAND - Passport required. Visa not required for stay up to 3 months. (Period begins when entering Scandinavian area: Denmark, Finland, Norway, Sweden.) For additional information, call Embassy of Iceland, 2022 Conn. Ave., N.W., Washington, D.C. 20008 (202/265-6653/5) or Consulate General in New York (212/686-4100).

INDIA - Passport and visa required. Obtain visa in advance. Tourist visa valid for stay up to 1 month, requires $5 fee, up to 6 months $25 fee and up to 12 months $50 fee, 1 application form, 2 photos, onward/return ticket and proof of sufficient funds. Visa must be obtained before arrival. Business visa requires $50 fee, 2 application forms, 2 photos and company letter stating purpose of trip. Include prepaid envelope for return of passport by certified mail. Allow 2 weeks for processing. Yellow fever immunization needed if arriving from infected area. AIDS test required for all students and anyone over 18 staying more than 1 year;

U.S. test sometimes accepted. Check requirements with Embassy of India, 2536 Mass Ave., N.W., Washington, D.C. 20008 (202/939-9839/9850) or nearest Consulate General: Chicago (312/781-6280), New York (212/879-7800) or San Francisco (415/668-0683).

INDONESIA - Valid passport and onward/return ticket required. Visa not required for tourist stay up to 2 months (non-extendable). For longer stays and additional information, consult Embassy of the Republic of Indonesia, 2020 Mass. Ave., N.W., Washington, D.C. 20036 (202/775-5200) or nearest Consulate: CA (213/383-5126 or 415/474-9571), IL (312/938-0101), NY (212/879-0600) or TX (713/626-3291).

IRAN - Passport and visa required. The United States does not maintain diplomatic or consular relations with Iran. Travel by U.S. citizens is not recommended. For visa information, contact Embassy of Pakistan,, Iranian Interests Section, 2209 Wisconsin Ave., NW, Washington, D.C., 20007 (202/965-4990).

IRAQ - Passport and visa required. AIDS test required for stay over 5 days. The United States suspended diplomatic and consular operation in Iraq since February 1991, **U.S. passports are not valid** for travel in, to, or through Iraq without authorization from the Department of State. Application for exemptions to this restriction should be submitted in writing to: Passport Services, U.S. Department of State, 1425 K St., N.W., Washington, D.C. 20524, Attn: CA/PPT/C, Room 300. **Attention:** U.S. citizens need a Treasury Dept. license in order to engage in any transactions related to travel to and within Iraq. Before planning any travel to Iraq, U.S. citizens should contact the Licensing Division, Office of Foreign Assets Control, Department of the Treasury, 1331 G St., N.W., Washington, D.C. 20220 (202/622-2480). For visa information, contact a country that maintains diplomatic relations with Iraq.

IRELAND - Passport required. Tourists are not required to obtain visa for stays under 90 days, but may be asked to show onward/return ticket. For further information, consult Embassy of Ireland, 2234 Mass. Ave., N.W., Washington, D.C. 20008 (202/462-3939) or nearest Consulate General: CA (415/392-4214), IL (312/337-1868), MA (617/267-9330) or NY (212/319-2555).

ISRAEL - Passport, onward/return ticket and proof of sufficient funds required. Tourist visa issued upon arrival valid for 3 months, but can be renewed. Obtain visa in advance if traveling on official/diplomatic passport. Departure tax $11 payable at airport ($160 dual nationals). Consult Embassy of Israel, 3514 International Dr., N.W., Washington, D.C. 20008 (202/364-5500) or nearest Consulate General: CA (213/651-5700 and 415/398-8885), FL (305/358-8111), GA (404/875-7851), IL (312/565-3300), MA (617/542-0041), NY (212/351-5200), PA (215/546-5556) or TX (713/627-3780).

ITALY - Passport required. Visa not required for tourist stay up to 3 months or longer stays, employment of study, obtain visa in advance. For additional information consult Embassy of Italy, Fuller St., N.W., Washington, D.C. 20009 (202/328-5500) or nearest Consulate General: CA (213/820-0622 or 415/931-4924), IL (312/467-1550), LA (514/524-2272), MA (617/542-0483), NY (212/737-9100), PA (215/592-7369) or TX (713/850-7520).

IVORY COAST - (See Cote D'lvoire.)

JAMAICA - If traveling directly from the United States, Puerto Rico, or the U.S. Virgin Islands, U.S. citizens need return/onward ticket, proof of U.S. citizenship, photo ID and proof of sufficient funds. Tourist card issued on arrival for stay up to 6 months; must be returned to immigration authorities on departure. For business or study, visa must be obtained in advance, no charge. Departure tax $15 paid at airport. Check information with Embassy of Jamaica, Suite 355, 1850 K St., N.W., Washington, D.C. 20006 (202/452-0660) or nearest Consulate: CA (213/380-9471 or 415/886-6061), FL (305/374-8431), GA (404/593-1500), IL (312/663-0023) or NY (212/935-9000).

JAPAN-Passport and onward/return ticket required. Visa not required for tourist/business stay up to 90 days. For official/ diplomatic travel visa required and must be obtained in advance, no charge. Departure tax $15.50 paid at airport. For specific information, consult Embassy of Japan, 2520 Mass. Ave., N.W., Washington, D.C. 20008 (202/939-6800) or nearest Consulate: AK (907/279-8428), CA (213/624-8305 or 415/777-3533), FL (305/530-9090) GA (404/892-2700), Guam (671/646-1290), Hl (808/536-2226), IL (312/280-0400), LA (504/529-2101), MA (617/973-9772), MO (816/471-0111), NY (212/371-8222), OR 9503/221-1811), TX (713/652-2977) or WA (206/68291 07).

JORDAN - Passport and visa required. Multiple-entry visa valid up to 5 years, no charge, requires 1 application form, 1 photo, letter stating purpose of visit and itinerary. Entry into Jordan sometimes denied to persons holding

passports with Israeli visa stamps. Send SASE for return
of passport by mail. For details check Embassy of the
Hashemite Kingdom of Jordan, 3504 International Dr.,
N.W., Washington, D.C. 20008 (202/966-2664).

KAZAKHSTAN - Passport and visa required. For
additional information contact Consular Section of the
Embassy of Russia, 1825 Phelps Pl., N.W., Washington,
D.C. 20008 (202/939-8907)or the Consulate General: San
Francisco (415/202-9800).

KENYA - Passport and visa required. Visa must be
obtained in advance. Single-entry visa for
tourist/business stay up to 6 months, $10; requires 1
application form, 2 photos and onward/return ticket.
Anti-malaria pills are recommended for those traveling
to the western or coastal regions. Yellow fever and
cholera immunizations recommended. Multiple-entry
visa for up to 1 year available, $50. Payment by money
order or cashier's check only. Airport departure tax $20.
Consult Embassy of Kenya, 2249 R St., N .W.,
Washington, D.C. 20008 (202/387-6101) or Consulate
General: Los Angeles (310/274-6635) or New York
(212/486-1300).

KIRIBATI (formerly Gilbert Islands) - Passport and visa
required. For additional information consult British
Embassy (202/462-1340).

KOREA, DEMOCRATIC PEOPLE'S REPUBLIC OF (North
Korea) - The United States does not maintain diplomatic
or consular relations with North Korea and has no third
country representing U.S. interests there. **Attention:** U.S.
citizens need a Treasury Dept. license in order to engage

in any transactions related to travel to and within North Korea. Before planning any travel to North Korea, U.S. citizens should contact the Licensing Division, Office of Foreign Assets Control, Department of the Treasury, 1331 G St., N.W., Washington, D.C. 20220 (202/622-2450). Visa information must be obtained from a consulate in a country that maintains diplomatic relations with North Korea.

KOREA, REPUBLIC OF (South Korea) - Passport required. Visa not required for a tourist stay up to 15 days. For longer stays and other types of travel, visa must be obtained in advance. Tourist visa for longer stay requires 1 application form and 1 photo. Business visa requires application form, 1 photo and company letter. Multiple-entry visa normally valid 5 years for visits up to 90 days requires 1 application form, 1 photo and affidavit of support. Fine imposed for overstaying visa and for long-term visa holders not registered within 60 days after entry. For further information check Embassy of the Republic of Korea (Consular Division), 2600 Virginia Ave., N.W., Suite 208, Washington, D.C. 20037 (202/939-5660/63) or nearest Consulate General: CA (213/385-9300 and 415/921-2251), GA (404/522-1611), IL (312/822-9485), MA (617/348-3660), NY (212/752-1700), TX (713/961-0186) or WA (206/441-1011) .

KUWAIT - Passport and visa required. AIDS test required for stay over 6 months; U.S. test accepted. For further information contact the Embassy of the State of Kuwait, 2940 Tilden St., N.W., Washington, D.C. 20008 (202/966-0702) or Consulate, 321 East 44th St., New York, N.Y. 10017 (212/973-4318).

KYRGYZSTAN - Passport and visa required. For additional information, contact Consular section of the Embassy of Russia, 1825 Phelps Pl., N.W., Washington, D.C. 20008 (202/939-8907) or the Consulate General: San Francisco (415/202-9800).

LAOS - Passport and visa required. Visa requires $35 fee, 3 application forms, 3 photos, onward/return transportation, sufficient funds, cholera immunization and SASE for return of passport by mail. Transit visas for stay up to 5 days requires onward return ticket and visa for next destination. Visitor visas are issued for 1 entry and must be within three months of the issue date. Period of stay: 1 month, can be extended for another 30 days (visitor visa application must be accompanied by letter from friend or relative). tourist visas are issued only to those who apply through a tourist agency. Business visa requires letter from counterpart in Laos and is valid for 1 entry and must be used within 3 months of issue date. Period of stay: 1 month, can be extended for another 30 days. Check information with Embassy of the Lao People's Democratic Republic, 2222 S St., N.W., Washington, D.C. 20008 (202/332-6416/7).

LATVIA - Passport and visa required. Tourist/business visas issued at Embassy or point of entry. For further information, contact Embassy of Latvia, 4325-17th St., N.W., Washington, D.C. 20011 (202, 726-8213).

LEBANON - Passport and visa required. Since January **1987, U.S. passports are not valid** for travel in, to, or through Lebanon without authorization from the Department of State. Application for exemptions to this restriction should be submitted in writing to Passport

Services, U.S. Department of State 1425 K St., N.W., Washington, D.C. 20524, Attn: CA/PPT/C Room 300. For further information contact Embassy of Lebanon, 2560-28th St., N.W., Washington, D.C. 20008 (202/ 939-6300) or nearest Consulate General: Los Angeles (213/ 467-1253), Detroit (313/567-0233) or New York (212/744-7905).

LEEWARD ISLANDS - (See Virgin Islands, British.)

LESOTHO - Passport and visa required. Visa requires 1 form. Single entry visa requires $5 fee and multiple-entry $10. For longer stays and other types of travel, check Embassy of the Kingdom of Lesotho, 2511 Mass. Ave., N.W., Washington, D.C. 20008 (202/797-5533).

LIBERIA - Passport and visa required. Transit visitors with onward ticket can remain at airport up to 48 hours. Other travelers must obtain visas before arrival. Tourist/business entry visa valid 3 months, no fee, requires 2 application forms, 2 photos, cholera and yellow fever vaccinations and medical certificate to confirm that traveler is in good health and free of any communicable disease. Company letter needed for business visa. Include SASE for return of passport by mail. Obtain exit permit from immigration authorities upon arrival, 1 photo required. For business requirements, call Embassy of the Republic of Liberia, 5201 16th St., N.W., Washington, D.C. 20011 (202/723-0437 to 0440) or nearest Consulate: CA (213/277-7692), GA (404/753-4754), IL (312/643-8635), LA (504/523-7784), Ml (313/342-3900) or NY (212/687-1025).

LIBYA - Passport and visa required. AIDS test required for those seeking residence permits; U.S. test accepted. Since December 1981, **U.S. passports are not valid for**

travel, in, to or through Libya without authorization from the Department of State. Application for exemptions to this restriction should be submitted in writing to Passport Services, U.S. Department of State, 1425 K St., N.W., Washington, D.C. 20524, Attn: CA/PPT/C, Room 300. **Attention:** U.S. citizens need a Treasury Dept. license in order to engage in any transactions related to travel to and within Libya. Before planning any travel to Libya, U.S. citizens should contact the Licensing Division, Office of Foreign Assets Control, Department of the Treasury, 1331 G St., N.W., Washington, D.C. 20220 (202/622-2480). Application and inquiries for visas must be made through a country that maintains diplomatic relations with Libya.

LIECHTENSTEIN - Passport required. Visa not required for tourist/business stay up to 3 months. For further information, consult the Swiss Embassy (202/745-7900).

LITHUANIA - Passport and visa required. Visa requires 1 application form and $25 fee. For further information contact Embassy of Lithuania, 2622 16th St., N.W., Washington, D.C. 20009 (202/234-5860).

LUXEMBOURG - Passport required. Visa not required for tourist/business stay up to 3 months. For additional information contact Embassy of Luxembourg, 2200 Mass. Ave., N.W., Washington, D.C. 20008 (202/265-4171) or the nearest Consulate: CA (415/788-0816), FL (305/373 -1300),GA (404/952-1157), IL (312/726-0355), MO (816/ 474- 4761), NY (212/370-9850), OH (513/422-4697) or TX (214/746-7200).

MACAU - Passport required. Visa not required for visits

up to 60 days. For further information, consult nearest Portuguese Consulate: Washington, D.C. (202/332-3007), San Francisco (415/346-3400), New Bedford (508/997-6151), Newark (201/622-7300), NY (212/246-4580), Providence (401/272-2003) or Portuguese Consulate in Hong Kong (231-338).

MACEDONIA - Macedonia has not been recognized as an independent country by the United States. U.S. citizens can obtain visas at the border.

MADAGASCAR - Passport and visa required. Visa valid 6 months for single-entry up to 90 days, $22.50 or multiple entries, $44.15 (no personal checks). Requires 4 application forms, 4 photos, yellow fever and cholera immunizations, proof of onward/return transportation and sufficient funds for stay. Include a prepaid envelope for return of passport by registered mail. Allow 4 months to process visa for longer stay. For additional information, contact Embassy of the Democratic Republic of Madagascar, 2374 Mass. Ave., N.W., Washington, D.C. 20008 (202/265-5525/6) or nearest Consulate: New York (212/986-9491), Philadelphia (215/893-3067) or Palo Alto, CA (415/323-7113).

MALAWI - Passport required. Visa not required for stay up to 1 year. Strict dress codes apply for anyone visiting Malawi. Women must wear dresses that cover their shoulders, arms and knees and may not wear slacks except in specifically designated areas. Men with long hair cannot enter the country. For further information about this and other requirements, contact the Embassy of Malawi, 2408 Mass. Ave., N.W., Washington, D.C. 20008 (202/797-1007) or Malawi Mission to the U.N., 600

3rd Ave., New York, N.Y. 10016 (212/949-0180).

MALAYSIA (and the Borneo States, Sarawak and Sabah)
- Passport required. Visa not required for stay up to 3 months. Yellow fever and cholera immunizations necessary if arriving from infected areas. For entry of pets or other types of visits, consult Embassy of Malaysia, 2401 Mass. Ave., N.W., Washington, D.C. 20008 (202/328-2700) or nearest Consulate: Los Angeles (213/621 -2991), New York (212/490-2722).

MALDIVES - Passport required. Tourist visa issued upon arrival, no charge. Visitors must have proof of onward/return transportation and sufficient funds (minimum of $10 per person per day of stay). Check with Embassy of Maldives in Sri Lanka for further information. The Embassy is located at 25 Melbourne Avenue, Colombo 4, Sri Lanka.

MALI - Passport and visa required. Visa must be obtained in advance. Tourist/business visa for stay up to 1 week, may be extended after arrival, requires $17 fee(cash or money order), 2 application forms, 2 photos, proof of onward/return transportation and yellow fever vaccination. Cholera immunization is recommended. For business travel, must have company letter stating purpose of trip. Send SASE for return of passport if applying by mail. Apply Embassy of the Republic of Mali, 2130 R St., N.W., Washington, D.C. 20008 (332-2249).

MALTA - Passport required. Visa not required for stay up to 3 months (extendable - extension must be applied for prior to end of three month period or expiration of original visa). Visa requires 3 application forms, 2 photos, and $25 fee (check or money order). For additional information consult Embassy of Malta, 2017 Conn. Ave., N.W., Washington, D.C. 20008 (202/462-3611/2) or nearest Consulate: CA(213/685-6365 and 415/468-4321), MA (617/742-1913), Ml (313/525-9777), MO (816/833-0033), MN (612/228-0935), NY (212/ 725-2345), PA (412/262-8460) or TX (713/497-2100).

MARSHALL ISLANDS, REPUBLIC OF THE - Proof of U.S. citizenship, sufficient funds for stay and onward/return ticket required for stay up to 30 days. Entry permit not needed to bring in sea-going vessel. Obtain necessary forms from airline or shipping agent serving Marshall Islands. Departure fee $10 (those over age 60 exempt). Health certificate required if arriving from infected areas. AIDS test may be required for visits over 30 days; U.S. test accepted. Check information with Representative Office, Suite 1004, 1901 Pennsylvania Ave., N.W., Washington, D.C. 20006 (202/ 234-5414) or office in Honolulu (808/942-4422).

MARTINIQUE - (See West Indies, French.)

MAURITANIA - Passport and visa required. Obtain visa before arrival. Visa valid 3 months, requires $10 fee (money order only), 2 application forms, 4 photos, yellow fever and cholera immunizations and proof of onward/return transportation. Business travelers must have proof of sufficient funds (bank statement) or letter from sponsoring company. For further information, contact Embassy of the Republic of Mauritania, 2129 Leroy Pl., N.W., Washington, D.C. 20008 (202/232-5700/01) or Permanent Mission to the U.N., 600 Third Ave., 37th Floor, New York, N.Y. 10016 (212/ 737-7780).

MAURITIUS - Passport, sufficient funds for stay and onward/ return ticket required. Visa not required for tourist/business stay up to 3 months. For travel on diplomatic/official passport, notify Embassy in advance of name, passport number and purpose of visit. For further information consult Embassy of Mauritius, Suite 441, 4301 Conn. Ave., N.W., Washington, D.C. 20008 (202/244-1491/2) or Honorary Consulate in Los Angeles (818/788-3720).

MAYOTTE ISLAND - (See France.)

MEXICO - Passport and visa not required of U.S. citizens for tourist transit stay up to 90 days. Tourist card is required. Tourist card valid 3 months for single entry up to 180 days, no charge, requires proof of U.S. citizenship, photo ID and proof of sufficient funds. Tourist cards may be obtained in advance from Consulate, Tourism Office, and most airlines serving Mexico upon arrival. Departure tax $10 is paid at airport. Notarized consent from parent(s) required for children traveling alone, with one parent or in someone else's custody. (This permit is not necessary when a minor is in possession of a valid passport.) For other types of travel and details, check Embassy of Mexico's Consular Section 2827 16th Street, NW, Washington, DC 20009-4260 (202/736-1000) or nearest Consulate General: CA (213/351-6800, 415/392-5554 and 619/231-8414), CO (303/830-6702), IL (312/855-1380), LA (504/522-3596), NY (212/ 689-0456), PR (809/764-0258) or TX (214/522-9741, 713/ 463-9426, 512/227-9145 and 915/533-3644).

MICRONESIA, FEDERATED STATES OF (Kosrae, Yap,

Ponape, and Truk) - Proof of citizenship, sufficient funds, onward/return ticket and identity required for tourist visit up to 6 months, extendable up to 12 months from date of entry after arrival in Micronesia. Departure fee $5. Entry permit may be needed for other types of travel; obtain forms from airline. Health certificate may be required if traveling from infected area. Typhoid and tetanus immunizations are recommended. AIDS test required for stay over 1 year. U.S. test accepted. For further information, contact Embassy of the Federated States of Micronesia, 1725 N St., N.W., Washington, D.C. 20036 (202/223-4383) or nearest consulate: Hawaii (808/836-4775) or Guam (671/646-9154).

MOLDOVA - Passport and visa required. For additional information contact the Consular Section of the Embassy of Russia, 1825 Phelps Place, N.W., Washington, D.C. 20008 (202/939-8907) or the Consulate General: San Francisco (415/202-9800).

MIQUELON ISLAND - Proof of U.S. citizenship and photo ID required for visit up to 3 months. For further information consult Embassy of France (202/944-6000).

MONACO - Passport required. Visa not required for visit up to 3 months. For further information consult French Embassy (202/944-6000) or nearest Honorary Consulate of the Principality of Monaco: CA (213/655-8970 or 415/362-5050), IL (312/642-1242), LA (504/522-5700), NY (212/759-5227) or PR (809/721-4215).

MONGOLIA - Passport and visa required. Transit visa for stay up to 48 hours requires onward ticket, visa for next destination and $20 fee ($40 for double transit). Tourist visa for up to 90 days requires confirmation from Mongolian Travel Agency (Zhuulchin) and $20 fee. Business visa requires letter from company stating purpose of trip and invitation from Mongolian organization and $20 fee ($60 multiple entry fee). Submit 1 application form, 2 photos, itinerary and prepaid envelope for return of passport by certified or special delivery mail. AIDS test required for students and anyone staying longer than 3 months; U.S. test accepted. For additional information contact Embassy of the People's Republic of Mongolia, 2833 M Street, NW, Washington, D.C., 20007 (202/333-7117).

MOROCCO - Passport required. Visa not required for stay up to 3 months, extendable. For additional information, consult Embassy of Morocco, 1601 21st St., N.W., Washington, D.C. 20009 (202/462-7979 to 7982) or Consulate General in New York (212/213-9644).

MOZAMBIQUE - Passport and visa required. Visa must be obtained in advance. Entry visa valid 30 days from date of issuance, requires 2 application forms, 2 photos, immunization for yellow fever and cholera, $15 fee and letter (from company or individual) giving detailed itinerary. Visitors must exchange $25 at point of entry and declare all foreign currency. Apply Embassy of the People's Republic of Mozambique, Suite 570, 1990 M St., N.W., Washington, D.C. 20036 (202/ 293-7146).

MYANMAR (formerly Burma) - Passport and visa required. Single entry visas, for stay up to 14 days, requires $16 fee for tourist visa and $30 fee for business visa, 2 application forms, 3 photos and itinerary. Tourist visas are issued for package or group tours as well as

Foreign Independent Travelers (FITs). FITs holding transit visas must change a minimum of U.S. $200 upon arrival. Overland travel into and out of Myanmar is not permitted. Enclose prepaid envelope for return of passport by registered/certified mail. Allow 2-3 weeks for processing. For further information contact Embassy of the Union of Myanmar, 2300 S St., N.W., Washington, D.C. 20008 (202/332-9044/6) or the Permanent Mission of Myanmar to the U.N., 10 East 77th St., New York, N.Y. 10021 (212/535-1311).

NAMIBIA - Passport, onward/return ticket and proof of sufficient funds required. Visa not required for tourist or business stay up to 90 days. Consult Embassy of Namibia, 1605 New Hampshire Ave., N.W., Washington, D.C. 20009 (202/986-0540) for further information on entry requirements.

NAURU - Passport and visa required. Passengers must have onward/return ticket. For specific information contact Consulate of the Republic of Nauru in Guam, First Floor, ADA Professional Bldg., Marine Drive, Agana, Guam 96910 (671/649-8300).

NEPAL - Passport and visa required. Tourist visa for stay up to 30 days issued at Katmandu Airport upon arrival, extendable to 3 months, requires $20 fee (postal money order), 1 application form and photo. For other types of travel obtain visa in advance. For additional information contact Royal Nepalese Embassy, 2131 Leroy Pl., N.W., Washington, D.C. 20008 (202/667-4550) or Consulate General in New York (212/370-4188).

NETHERLANDS - Passport required. Visa not required

for tourist/business visit up to 90 days. Tourists may be asked to show onward/return ticket or proof of sufficient funds for stay. For further information contact Embassy of the Netherlands, 4200 Linnean Ave., N.W., Washington, D.C. 20008 (202/244-5300) or nearest Consulate General: CA (213/380-3440), IL (312/856-0110), NY (212/ 246-1429) or TX (713/ 622-8000).

NETHERLAND ANTILLES - (Islands include Bonaire, Curacao, Saba, Statia, St. Martin [St. Maarten]) . Passport or proof of U.S. citizenship required. Visa not required for stay up to 14 days, extendable to 90 days after arrival. Tourists may be asked to show onward/return ticket or proof of sufficient funds for stay. Departure tax $10 when leaving Bonaire and Curacao, $4 in Statia, $10 in St. Martin. For further information, consult Embassy of the Netherlands (202/244-5300), or nearest Consulate General: CA (213/380-3440), IL (314/856-1429), NY (212/246-1429) or TX (713/622-8000).

NEW CALEDONIA - (See French Polynesia.)

NEW ZEALAND - Passport required. Visa not required for tourist/business stay up to 3 months, must have onward/return ticket and visa for next destination. Proof of sufficient funds may also be required. For additional information, contact Embassy of New Zealand, 37 Observatory Circle, N.W., Washington, D.C. 20008 (202/328-4800) or nearest Consulate General Los Angeles (213/477-8241).

NICARAGUA - Passport must be valid 6 months beyond duration of stay, onward/return ticket and sufficient funds ($200 minimum) required. Check further information with Embassy of Nicaragua, 1627 New Hampshire Ave., N.W. Washington, D.C. 20009 (202/939-6531 to 34).

NIGER - Passport and visa required. Visa valid between 7 and 12 months (from date of issuance), depending on type/category of travelers. Requires 3 application forms, 3 photos, yellow vaccinations (cholera vaccination is recommended, but not required), proof of onward/return transportation and letter of invitation. For further information, contact Embassy of the Republic of Niger, 2204 R St., N.W. Washington, D.C. 20008 (202/483-4224).

NIGERIA - Passport and visa required. Visa, no charge, valid for one entry within 12 months, requires 1 photo, yellow fever and cholera vaccinations, and for tourism a letter of invitation is required. Business visa requires letter from counterpart in Nigeria and letter of introduction from U.S. company. For further information, contact Embassy of the Republic of Nigeria, 2201 M St., N.W., Washington, D.C. 20037 (202/822-1500 or 1522) or the Consulate General: New York (212/ 715-7200).

NIUE - Passport, onward/return ticket and confirmed hotel accommodations required. Visa not required for stay up to 30 days. For additional information, consult Embassy of New Zealand (202/328-4800).

NORFOLK ISLAND - Passport and visa required. Visa issued upon arrival for visit of up to 30 days, extendable, requires confirmed accommodations and onward/return ticket. Australian transit visa must be obtained in advance for travel to Norfolk Island. For both visas, consult Australian Embassy (202/797-3000).

NORWAY - Passport required. Visa not required for stay up to 3 months. (Period begins when entering Scandinavian area: Finland, Sweden, Denmark, Iceland.) For further information, contact Royal Norwegian Embassy, 2720 34th St., N.W., Washington, D.C. 20008 (202/333-6000) or nearest Consulate General: CA (415/986-0766 to 7168 and 213/933-7717), MN (612/332-3338), NY (212/421-7333) or TX (713/521 -2900).

OMAN - Passport and visa required. Tourist/business visas for single-entry issued for stay up to 3 weeks. Requires $21 fee, 1 application form, 1 photo and cholera immunization if arriving from infected area. Allow 1 week to 10 days for processing. Entry not granted to passports showing Israeli or Libyan visas. For transit and road travel check Embassy of the Sultanate of Oman, 2342 Mass. Ave., N.W., Washington, D.C. 20008 (202/387-1980-2).

PAKISTAN - Passport and visa required. Visa must be obtained before arrival. Tourist visa requires 1 application form, 1 photo and proof of onward/return transportation. Validity depends on visit (minimum 3 months), multiple entries, no charge. Need letter from company for business visa. Include prepaid envelope for return of passport by registered mail. AIDS test required for stays over 1 year. For applications and inquiries in Washington area, contact Consular Section of the Embassy of Pakistan, 2315 Mass. Ave., N.W., Washington, D.C. 20008 ~202/ 939-6261). All other areas apply to Consulate General, 12 East 65th St., New York, N.Y. 10021 (212/879-5800).

PALAU, THE REPUBLIC OF - Proof of U.S. citizenship onward/return ticket required for stay up to 30 days (extendable). Must apply for extension in Palau, $50 fee. Obtain forms for entry permit from airline or shipping agent serving Palau. For further information, consult with Representative Office, 444 N. Capitol St., Suite 308, Washington, D.C. 20008 (202/624-7793).

PANAMA - Passport, tourist card or visa and onward/return ticket required. Tourist card available from airline serving Panama for $5 fee. For longer stays and official/diplomatic travel information, contact Embassy of Panama, 2862 McGill Terrace, N.W., Washington, D.C. 20008 (202/483-1407).

PAPUA NEW GUINEA - Passport required. Tourist/business visa issued upon arrival at Jackson's Airport (Port Moresby) for stays of 3 months or less. card valid 30 days. AIDS test required for work and residency permit; U.S. test accepted. For longer stays and further information, contact Embassy of Papua New Guinea, Suite 300, 1615 New Hampshire Ave., N.W., Washington, D.C. 20009 (202/745-3680).

PARAGUAY - Passport required. Visa not required for tourist/business stay up to 90 days (extendable). Health test required for resident visas. Visas required for diplomatic/official travel. Visa must be obtained in advance. For additional information, consult Embassy of Paraguay, 2400 Mass. Ave., N.W., Washington, D.C. 20008 (202/483-6960).

PERU - Passport required. Visa not required for tourist

stay up to 90 days, extendable after arrival. Tourists may need onward/return ticket. For official/diplomatic passport and other travel, visa required and must be obtained in advance. Business visa requires company letter stating purpose of trip and $27 fee. For further information contact Embassy of Peru, 1700 Mass. Ave., N.W., Washington, D.C. 20036 (202/833-9860-9) or nearest Consulate: CA (213/383-9896 and 415/ 362-5185), FL (305/374-1407), IL (312/853-6173), NJ (201/ 278-2221), NY (212/644-2850), PR (809/763-0679) or TX (713/781 -5000).

PHILIPPINES - Passport and onward/return ticket required. For entry by Manila International Airport, visa not required for transit tourist stay up to 21 days. Visa required for longer stay, maximum of 59 days, 1 application form, 1 photo, no charge. Company letter needed for business visa. AIDS test required for permanent residency; U.S. test accepted. For more information, check Embassy of the Philippines, 1617 Mass. Av., N.W., Washington, D.C. 20036 (202/483-1533) or nearest Consulate General: CA (213/387-5321 and (415/433-6666), Hl (808/595-6316), IL (312/3326458), NY (212/764-1330), TX (713/621-8609) or WA (206/441 -1640).

POLAND - Passport required. Visa not required for stay up to 90 days. Visitors must register at hotel or with local authorities within 48 hours after arrival. AIDS Test required for student visas; U.S. test accepted. Apply Embassy of the Republic of Poland (Consular Division), 2224 Wyoming Ave., N.W., Washington, D.C. 20008 (202/ 232-4517) or nearest Consulate General: Chicago, IL, 1530 Lakeshore Dr., 60610 (312/337-3816). Los Angeles, CA 3460 Wilshire Blvd., Suite 1200, 90010 (213/365-7900) or New York, N.Y., 233 Madison Ave., 10016 (212/889-8360).

PORTUGAL - (Includes travel to the Azores and Madeira Islands.) Passport required. Visa not required for visit up to 60 days (extendable). For travel with pets and other information, consult nearest Consulate: Washington, DC (202/332-3007), CA (415/ 346-3400), MA (617/536-8740 and 508/997-6151), NJ (201/622-7300), NY (212/246-4580) or RI (401/272-2003).

QATAR - Passport and visa required. Single-entry visa $33; multiple-entry visa, valid 3-6 months for $60 fee or 12 months for $115 fee; transit visa. $6. Visas require No Objection Certificate from Qatar Ministry of the Interior, 2 application forms, 2 photos and SASE for return of passport by mail. Business visa must be obtained through sponsor in Qatar. AIDS test required for work and student visas; U.S. test accepted if within 3 months of visit . For specific information contact Embassy of the State of Qatar, Suite 1180, 600 New Hampshire Ave., N.W., Washington, D.C. 20037 (202/338-0111).

REUNION - (See France.)

ROMANIA - Passport and visa required. Transit and tourist visa may be obtained at border in Romania or from Romanian Embassy or Consulate before departure. Transit/business/single entry visa valid 6 months for stay up to 60 days, requires $31 fee (multiple-entry, $68). No application or photos needed. Provide SASE for return of passport by mail. Allow 1-3 days for processing For additional information, family visits and other information contact Embassy of Romania, 1607 23rd St., N.W., Washington, D.C. 20008 (202/232-4747-9) or the Consulate General, New York (212/682-9120, 9121, 9122).

RUSSIA - Passport and visa required. Tourist visa, no charge, requires 1 application form, 3 photos, confirmation from tourist agency in the Commonwealth of Independent States (CIS) and processing fee (visa processing fee is $20 for 2 weeks, $30 for one week and $60 for three days processing time). Business visa requires 1 application, 3 photos, and letter of invitation from a CIS company. Multiple-entry business visa $120 plus processing fee. Fee paid by money order or company check only. For additional information, contact the Consular Section of the Embassy of Russia, 1825 Phelps Place, N.W, Washington, D.C. 20008 (202/939-8907, 8911 and 8913) or the Consulate General: San Francisco (415/202-9800).

RWANDA - Passport and visa required. Multiple-entry visa for stay up to 3 months requires, $15 fee, 2 application forms, 2 photos and immunizations for yellow fever. Exact date of entry into Rwanda required with application. Include prepaid envelope or postage for return of passport by certified mail. Apply at one of the following: Embassy of the Republic of Rwanda, 1714 New Hampshire Ave., N.W., Washington, D.C. 20009 (202/232-2882), Permanent Mission of Rwanda to the U.N., 124 East 39th Street, New York, N. Y. 10016 (212/696-0644/45/46) or the Consulate General in Chicago (708/205-1188) or Denver (303/321-2400).

SAINT KITTS AND NEVIS - Proof of U.S. citizenship, photo ID and return/onward ticket required for stay up to 6 months. AIDS test required for work permit, residency or student visas; U.S. test is accepted. For further information, consult Embassy of St. Kitts and Nevis, 2501

M St., N.W., Washington, D.C. 20037 (202/833-3550) or Permanent Mission to the U.N., 414 East 75th St., Fifth Floor, New York, N.Y. 10021 (212/535-1234).

SAINT LUCIA - Passport (or proof of U.S. citizenship and photo ID) and return/ onward ticket required for stay up to 6 months. For additional information contact Embassy of Saint Lucia, 2100 M St., N.W., Suite 309, Washington, D.C. 20037 (202/463-7378/9) or Permanent Mission to the U.N., 820 Second St., 9th Floor, New York, N.Y. 10017 (212/697-9360).

ST. MARTIN (St. Maarten) - (See Netherlands Antilles or West Indies, French.).

ST. PIERRE - Proof of U.S. citizenship and photo ID required for visit up to 3 months. For specific information, consult Embassy of France (202/944-6000).

SAINT VINCENT AND THE GRENADINES - Proof of U.S. citizenship, photo ID and return/onward ticket and/or proof of sufficient funds required for tourist stay up to 6 months.   For more information consult the Embassy of Saint Vincent and the Grenadines, 1717 Mass. Ave., N.W., Suite 102, Washington, D.C. 20036 (202/462-7806 or 7846) or Consulate, 801 Second Ave., 21st Floor, New York, N.Y. 10017 (212/687-4490).

SAN MARINO - Passport required. Visa not required for tourist stay up to 3 months. For additional information, contact the nearest Honorary Consulate of the Republic of San Marino: Washington, D.C. (1155 21st St., N.W., Suite 400, Washington, D.C. 20036, 202/223-3517), Detroit (313/528-1190) or New York (212/736-3911).

SAO TOME AND PRINCIPE - Passport and visa required. Tourist/business visa for visit up to 2 weeks, requires 2 application forms, 2 photos and yellow fever immunization card, letter stating purpose of travel and $12 fee. Company letter is required for a business visa. Enclose prepaid envelope or postage for return of passport by certified or special delivery mail. Apply Permanent Mission of Sao Tome and Principe to the U.N., 122 East 42nd Street, Suite 1604, New York, N.Y. 10168 (212/697-4211).

SAUDI ARABIA - Passport and visa required. (Tourist visa are not available for travel to Saudi Arabia.). Transit visa valid 24 hours for stay in airport, need onward/return ticket. Business visa requires $15 fee (money order only), 1 application form, 1 photo, company letter stating purpose of visit, invitation from Foreign Ministry in Saudi Arabia and SASE for return of passport by mail. Meningitis and cholera vaccinations are highly recommended. Medical report, including AIDS test, required for work permits; U.S. test accepted. For details and requirements for family visits, contact The Royal Embassy of Saudi Arabia, 601 New Hampshire Ave., N.W., Washington, D.C . 20037 (202/333-4595) or nearest Consulate General: Los Angeles (213/208-6566), New York (212/752-2740) or Houston (713/785-5577).

SCOTLAND - (See United Kingdom.)

SENEGAL - Passport required. Visa not needed for stay up to 90 days. U.S. citizens need onward/return ticket and yellow fever vaccination. For further information contact Embassy of the Republic of Senegal, 2112 Wyoming Ave., N.W., Washington, D.C. 20008 (202/234-0540).

SERBIA AND MONTENEGRO - Passport required. For further information check with the Office of the Federal Republic of Yugoslavia, 2410 California St., N.W., Washington, D.C. 2008 (202/462-6566). <u>Attention</u>: U.S. citizens need a Treasury Dept. License in order to engage in any commercial transactions within Serbia & Montenegro. Before planning any travel to Serbia & Montenegro, U.S. citizens should contact the Licensing Division, Office of Foreign Assets Control, Department of the Treasury, 1331 G St., N.W., Washington, D.C. 20220 (202/6622-2480).

SEYCHELLES - Passport, onward/return ticket and proof of sufficient funds required. Visa issued upon arrival for stay up to 1 month, no charge, extendable up to 1 year. Consult Permanent Mission of Seychelles to the U.N., 820 Second Ave., Suite 203, New York, N.Y. 10017 (212/687-9766) for further information.

SIERRA LEONE - Passport and visa required. Single-entry visa valid 3 months, 1 application form, 1 photo, return/onward ticket and proof of financial support from bank or employer. Cholera and yellow fever immunizations required and malarial suppressants recommended. Adult travelers (over age 16) must exchange $100 minimum upon arrival and declare other foreign currency on an exchange control form (M), certified and stamped at the port of entry. For further information, consult Embassy of Sierra Leone, 1701 19th St., N.W., Washington, D.C. 20009 (202/939-9261).

SINGAPORE - Passport and onward/return ticket required. Visa not required for tourist/business stay up to 2 weeks, extendable to 3 months maximum. Foradditional information, contact Embassy of Singapore, 1824 R St., N.W., Washington, D.C. 20009 (202/667-7555).

SLOVAK REPUBLIC - Passport required. Visa not required for stay up to 30 days. For longer stays and other types of travel contact Embassy of the Slovak Republic, 3900 Spring of Freedom Street, N.W., Washington, D.C. 20008 (202/363-6315).

SLOVENIA - Passport and visa required. Visas are not available in the U.S. Travelers can obtain tourist visas (no charge) at entry point. Additional information can be obtained from the Embassy of Slovenia, 1300 19th St., N.W., Washington, D.C. 20036 (202/828-1650).

SOLOMON ISLANDS - Passport, onward/return ticket and proof of sufficient funds required. Visitors permit issued on arrival for stay up to 2 months in 1-year period. For further information consult British Embassy (202/462-1340).

SOMALIA - Passport and visa required. For further information contact Consulate of the Somali Democratic Republic in New York (212/688-9410).

SOUTH AFRICA - Passport and visa required. Visa must be obtained in advance. Multiple-entry visa valid 1 year if passport remains valid, no charge, requires 1 application form (no photo), proof of onward/return transportation, visa for next destination, itinerary and yellow fever vaccination if arriving from infected area. Malarial suppressants also recommended. Enclose prepaid envelope or postage for return of passport by certified or express mail. Allow 2-3 weeks for processing. For business travel, a company letter is required. For more information contact: Embassyof South Africa, Attn: Consular Office, 3201 New Mexico Ave., N.W., Washington, D.C. 20016 (202/966-1650) or nearest Consulate: CA (310/657-9200), IL (312/939-7929) or NY (212/213-4880).

SPAIN - Passport required. Visa not required for tourist stay up to 6 months. If traveling on diplomatic/official passport, visa required and must be obtained in advance. For additional information check with Embassy of Spain, 2700 15th St., N.W., Washington, D.C. 20009 (202/265-0190/1) or nearest Consulate General: CA (415/922-2995 and 213/658-6050), FL (305/446-5511), IL (312/782-4588), LA (504/525-4951), MA (617/536-2506), NY (212/355-4080), PR (809/758-6090) or TX (713/783-6200).

SRI LANKA - Passport, onward/return ticket and proof of sufficient funds ($15 per day) required. Tourist visa not required for stay up to 90 days. For business or travel on official/diplomatic passport, visa required and must be obtained in advance. Business visa valid 1 month, requires 1 application form, 2 photos, a company letter, a letter from sponsoring agency in Sri Lanka, a copy of an onward/return ticket, and $5 fee. Include $6 postage for return of passport by registered mail. Yellow fever and cholera immunizations needed if arriving from infected area. For further information contact Embassy of the Democratic Socialist Republic of Sri Lanka, 2148 Wyoming Ave., N.W., Washington, D.C. 20008 (202/483-

4025) or nearest Consulate: CA (805/323-8975 and 504/362-3232), HI (808/373-2040), or NJ (201/627-7855), or NY (212/986-7040).

SUDAN - Passport and visa required. Visa must be obtained in advance. Transit visa valid up to 7 days, requires $6 fee (cash or money order), onward/return ticket and visa for next destination, if appropriate. Tourist/business visa for single entry up to 3 months (extendable), requires $9 fee, 1 application form, 1 photo, proof of sufficient funds for stay and SASE for return passport. Business visa requires company letter stating purpose of visit and invitation from Sudanese officials. Malarial suppressants and vaccinations for yellow fever, cholera, and meningitis recommended. Visas not granted to passports showing Israeli or South African visas. Allow 4 weeks for processing. Travelers must declare currency upon arrival and departure. Check additional currency regulations for stay longer than 2 months. Contact Embassy of the Republic of the Sudan, 2210 Mass. Ave., N.W., Washington, D.C. 20008 (202/338-8565 to 8570) or Consulate General, 210 East 49th St., New York, N.Y. 10017 (212/421-2680).

SURINAME - Passport and visa required. Multiple-entry visa requires 2 application forms, 2 photos. Business visa requires letter from sponsoring company. For return of passport by mail, send $5 for registered mail, or $9.95 for Express Mail. For additional information and other requirements, contact Embassy of the Republic of Suriname, Suite 108, 4301 Conn. Ave., N.W., Washington D.C. 20008 (202/244-7488 and 7490) or the Consulate: Miami (305/593-2163).

SWAZILAND - Passport required. Visa not required for stay up to 60 days. Temporary residence permit available in Mbabane for longer stay. Visitors must report to immigration authorities or police station within 48 hours unless lodging in a hotel. Yellow fever and cholera immunizations required if arriving form infected area and anti-malarial treatment recommended. For further information consult Embassy of the Kingdom of Swaziland, 3400 International Dr., N.W., Suite 3M, Washington, D.C. (202/362-6683).

SWEDEN - Valid passport required. Visa not required for stay up to 3 months. (Period begins when entering Scandinavian area: Finland, Norway, Denmark, Iceland.) For further information check Embassy of Sweden, Suite 1200, 600 New Hampshire Ave., N.W., Washington, D.C. 20037 (202/944-5600) or nearest Consulate General: Los Angeles (310/575-3383), Chicago (312/781-6262)or New York (212/751-5900).

SWITZERLAND - Passport required. Visa not required for tourist/business stay up to 3 months. For further information contact Embassy of Switzerland, 2900 Cathedral Ave., N.W, Washington, D.C. 20008 (202/745-7900) or nearest Consulate General: CA (310/575-1145 or 415/788-2272), GA (404/872-7874), IL (312/915-0061), NY (212/758-2560) or TX (713/650-0000).

SYRIA - Passport and visa required. Obtain visa in advance. Single-entry visa valid 6 months or double-entry for 3 months, $15; multiple-entry visa valid 6 months, $30. Submit 2 application forms, 2 photos (signed) and fee (payment must be money order only). Enclose prepaid envelope (with correct postage) for return of passport by mail. AIDS test required for students and others staying over 1 year; U.S. test sometimes accepted. For group visas and other information, contact Embassy of the Syrian Arab Republic, 2215 Wyoming Ave., N.W., Washington, D.C. 20008 (202/232-6313).

TAHITI - (See French Polynesia.)

TAIWAN - Passport and visa required. Visas for stay up to 2 months, no charge, requires 1 application form, onward/return ticket and 2 photos. AIDS test mandatory for anyone staying over 3 months; U.S. test sometimes accepted. For business travel or other information, contact Coordination Council for North American Affairs (CCNAA), 4201 Wisconsin Avenue, N.W., Washington, D.C. 20016-2137 (202/895-1800). Additional offices are in Atlanta, Boston, Chicago, Guam, Honolulu, Houston, Kansas City, Los Angeles, New York, San Francisco, and Seattle.

TAJIKISTAN - Passport and visa required. For additional information contact the Consular Section of the Russian Embassy 1825 Phelps Place, N .W., Washington, D.C. 20008 (202/939-8907, 8911 or 8913) or the Consulate General: San Francisco (415/202-9800).

TANZANIA - Passport and visa required. Obtain visa before departure. Visas for mainland Tanzania are valid for Zanzibar. Tourist visa (valid 6 months from date of issuance) for 1 entry up to 30 days, may be extended after arrival. Requires $10.50 fee (no personal checks). Enclose prepaid envelope for return of passport by certified or registered mail. Visitors must exchange at least $50 at point of entry. Yellow fever and cholera immunizations recommended (required if arriving from infected area) and malarial suppressants advised. Allow 1 month for processing. For business visa and other information, consult Embassy of the United Republic of Tanzania, 2139 R St., N.W., Washington, D.C. 20008 (202/939-6125) or Tanzanian Permanent Mission to the U.N. 205 East 42nd St., 13th Floor, New York, N.Y. 10017 (212/972-9160).

THAILAND - Passport and onward/return ticket required. Visa not needed for stay up to 15 days if arrive and depart from Don Muang Airport in Bangkok. For longer stays, obtain visa in advance. Transit visa or stay up to 30 days, $10 fee or tourist visa for stay up to 60 days, $15 fee. For business visa valid up to 90 days, need $20 fee and company letter stating purpose of visit. Submit 1 application form, 2 photos and postage for return of passport by mail. Apply Embassy of Thailand, 2300 Kalorama Rd., N .W., Washington, D.C. 20008 (202/234-5052) or nearest Consulate General: CA (213/937-1894), IL(312/236-2447) or NY (212/754-1770).

TOGO - Passport required. Visa not required for stay up to 3 months. Americans traveling in remote areas in Togo occasionally require visas. Yellow fever and cholera vaccinations are required. Check further information, with Embassy of the Republic of Togo, 2208 Mass. Ave., N.W., Washington, D.C. 20008 (202/234-4212/3).

TONGA - Passport and onward/return ticket required. Visa not required for stay up to 30 days. For additional information, consult the Consulate General of Tonga, 360 Post St., Suite 604, San Francisco, CA 94108 (415/781-0365).

TRINIDAD AND TOBAGO - Passport required. Visa not required for tourist/business stay up to 2 months. If traveling on official/diplomatic passport or for other travel, visa required and must be obtained in advance. Business visa requires passport and company letter. For further information, consult Embassy of Trinidad and Tobago, 1708 Mass Ave., N.W., Washington, D.C. 20036 (202/467-6490) or nearest Consulate in New York (212/682-7272).

TUNISIA - Passport and onward/return ticket required. Visas not required for tourist/business stay up to 4 months. For further information, consult Embassy of Tunisia, 1515 Mass. Ave., N.W., Washington, D.C. 20005 (202/862-1850) or nearest Consulate: San Francisco (415/922-9222) or New York (212/272-6962).

TURKEY - Passport required. Visa not required for tourist business stay up to 3 months. If traveling on official/diplomatic passport or for other travel, visa required and must be obtained in advance. For further information, contact Embassy of the Republic of Turkey, 1714 Mass. Ave., N.W., Washington, D.C. 20036 (202/659-0742) or nearest Consulate: CA (213/937-0118),IL (312/263-0644), NY(212/949-0160) or TX (713/622-5849).

TURKMENISTAN - Passport and visa required. For additional information, contact the Consular Section of the Russian Embassy, 1825 Phelps Place, N.W., Washington, D.C. 20008 (202/939-8907, 8911 or 8913) or the Consulate General: San Francisco (415/202-9800).

TURKS AND CAICOS - (See West Indies, British.)

TUVALU - Passport and onward/return ticket and proof of sufficient funds required. Visitors permit issued on arrival. For further information, consult British Embassy (202/462-1340).

UGANDA - Passport and visa required. Obtain visa before arrival. Visas, valid within 3 months to 6 months, $20 fee (money order), requires 2 application forms, 2 photos. Immunization certificates for yellow fever, cholera, typhoid and malaria suppressants are required as well. For business visa and other information, contact Embassy of the Republic of Uganda, 5909 16th St., N.W., Washington, D.C. 20011 (202/726-7100-02) or Permanent Mission to the U.N. (212/949-0110).

UKRAINE - Passport and visa required. Visas may be obtained at the Ukraine Embassy in the U.S., at airports in Ukraine, or at any border crossing point. Visa requires 1 application, 1 photo and $50 fee (company check or money order only). Processing time is approximately 9 business days. For additional information, contact Embassy of Ukraine, Suite 711, 1828 L Street, N.W., Washington, D.C. 20036 (202/296-6960).

UNITED ARAB EMIRATES - Passport and visa required. Tourist visa must be obtained by relative/sponsor in UAE. Transit visa issued upon arrival at discretion of airport authorities for stay up to 15 days. Both visas require sponsor/relative to meet visitor at airport. Business visas issued only by Embassy, and require company letter and sponsor in UAE to send a fax or telex to Embassy confirming trip. Single-entry visa valid 2 months for stay up to 30 days, $18 fee. Multiple entry visa (for business only), valid 6 months from date of issue for maximum stay of 30 days per entry, $225 fee, paid by cash, money order or certified check. Submit 2 application forms, 2 photos and prepaid envelope for return of passport by certified/registered mail. AIDS test required for work or residence permits; testing must be performed upon arrival; U.S. test not accepted. For further information, contact Embassy of the United Arab Emirates, Suite 740, 600 New Hampshire Ave., N.W., Washington, D.C. 20037 (202/338-6500).

UNITED KINGDOM (England, Northern Ireland, Scotland, and Wales) - Passport required. Visa not required for stay up to 6 months. For additional information, consult the Consular Section of the British Embassy, 19 Observatory Circle, N.W., Washington, D.C. 20008 (202/896-0205) or nearest Consulate General: CA (213/385-7381 and 415/981-3030), GA (404/524-5856), IL (312/346-1810), MA (617/437-7160), NY (212/752-8400), OH (216/621-7674) or TX (214/637-3600).

URUGUAY - Passport required. Visa not required to stay up to 3 months. For additional information, consult Embassy of Uruguay, 1918 F St., N.W., Washington, D.C. 20008 (202/331-1313-6) or nearest Consulate: CA (213/394-5777), FL (305/358-9350), IL (312/236-3366), LA (504/525-8354) or NY (212/753-8191/2).

UZBEKISTAN - Passport and visa required. For additional information, contact the Consular Section of the Russian Embassy, 1825 Phelps Place, N.W., Washington, D.C. 20008 (202/939-8907, 8911 or 8913) or the Consulate General: San Francisco (415/202-9800).

VANUATU - Passport and onward/return ticket

required. Visa not required for stay up to 30 days. For further information, consult the British Embassy (202/462-1340).

VATICAN - (See Holy See.)

VENEZUELA - Passport and tourist card required. Tourist card can be obtained from airlines serving Venezuela, no charge, valid 60 days, cannot be extended. Multiple-entry visa valid up to 1 year, extendable, available from any Venezuelan Consulate, requires $30 fee (money order or company check), 1 application form, 1 photo, onward/return ticket, proof of sufficient funds and certification of employment. For business visa, need letter from company stating purpose of trip, responsibility for traveler and name and address of companies to be visited in Venezuela. All travelers must pay departure tax ($12) at airport. Business travelers must present a Declaration of Income Tax in the Ministerio de Hacienda (Treasury Department). For additional information, contact the Consular Section of the Embassy of Venezuela, 1099 30th Street, N.W., Washington, D.C. 20007 (202/342-2214) or the nearest consulate: CA (415/512-8340), FL (305/577-3834), IL (312/236-9655), LA (504/522-3284), MA (617/266-9355), NY(212/826-1660), PA (215/923-2905), PR (809/766-4250) or TX (713/961-5141).

VIETNAM - The United States does not maintain diplomatic or consular relations with Vietnam and has no third country representing U.S. interests there. Travel is not recommended by U.S. citizens. **Attention:** U.S. citizens need a Treasury Dept. license in order to engage in any transactions related to travel to and within Vietnam. Before planning any travel to Vietnam, U.S.

citizens should contact the Licensing Division, Office of Foreign Assets Control, Department of the Treasury, 1331 G St., N.W., Washington, D.C. 20220 (202/622-2480). Visa must be obtained from consulate in a country that maintains diplomatic relations with Vietnam.

VIRGIN ISLANDS, British - Islands include Anegarda, Jost van Dyke, Tortola and Virgin Gorda. Proof of U.S. citizenship, photo ID, onward/return ticket and sufficient funds required for tourist stay up to 3 months. AIDS test required for residency or work; U.S. test accepted. Consult British Embassy for further information (202/462-1340).

WALES - (See United Kingdom.)

WEST INDIES, British - Islands include Anguilla, Montserrat, Cayman Islands, Turks and Caicos. Proof of U.S. citizenship, photo ID, onward/return ticket and sufficient funds required for tourist stay up to 3 months. AIDS test required for residency or work; U.S. test accepted. Consult British Embassy for further information (202/462-1340).

WEST INDIES, French - Islands include Guadeloupe, Isles des Saintes, La Desirade, Marie Galante, Saint Barthelemy, St. Martin and Martinique. Proof of U.S. citizenship and photo ID required for visit up to 3 weeks. (For stays longer than 3 weeks a passport is required.) No visa required for stay up to 3 months. For further information consult Embassy of France (202/944-6000/6215).

WESTERN SAMOA- Passport and onward/return ticket required. Visa not required for stay up to 30 days. For longer stays, contact Western Samoa Mission to the U.N., 820 2nd Avenue, Suite 800, New York, N.Y. (212/599-6190 or 96).

YEMEN ARAB REPUBLIC - Passport and visa required. Visa valid 30 days from date of issuance for single entry, requires 1 application form and 2 photos . For tourist visa, you need proof of onward/return transportation and employment and $20 fee. Visitors visa requires letter of invitation and $20 fee. Business visa requires $20, company letter stating purpose of trip. Payment by money order only and include postage for return of passport by registered mail. Entry not granted to passports showing Israeli or South African visa. Yellow fever and cholera vaccinations and malaria suppressants recommended. Check information with Embassy of the Republic Yemen, Suite 705, 2600 Virginia Ave., N.W., Washington, D.C. 20037 (202/965-4760) or Yemen Mission to the U.N., 866 United Nations Plaza, Rm. 435, New York, N.Y. 10017 (212/355-1730).

ZAIRE - Passport and visa required. Visa must be obtained before arrival. Transit visa for stay up to 8 days. single-entry $8; double-entry $16. Tourist visa, valid 1 month $20; 2 months $40 and 3 months $50, requires 3 photos, 3 applications, yellow fever immunization and onward/return ticket. Business visa valid 6 months, $60, need company letter accepting financial responsibility for traveler. No personal checks, send money order and enclose SASE for return of passport by mail. Apply Embassy of the Republic of Zaire, 1800 New Hampshire Ave., N.W., Washington, D.C. 20009 (202/234-7690/1) or Permanent Mission to the U. N., 747 Third Ave., New York, N.Y. 10017 (212/754-1966).

ZAMBIA - Passport and visa required. Obtain visa in advance. Visa valid up to 6 months, requires $10 fee (no personal checks), 2 application forms and 2 photos. Business visa also require company letter. Yellow fever and cholera immunizations recommended.   Apply Embassy of the Republic of Zambia, 2419 Mass. Ave., N.W., Washington, D.C. 20008 (202/265-9717-21).

ZANZIBAR - (See Tanzania.)

ZIMBABWE - Passport, onward/return ticket and proof of sufficient funds required.   Visitors must declare currency upon arrival.   For regulations, check with Embassy of Zimbabwe, 1608 New Hampshire Ave., N.W., D.C. 20009 (202/332-7100).

TRAVEL RESOURCES WE RECOMMEND

We highly recommend joining an organization called **The International Association of Air Travel Couriers**. $35 per year buys you a host of services and items:

- Two bi-monthly newsletters, The *Shoestring Traveler* (tips and experiences gleaned from couriers) and the *Air Courier Bulletin. The Air Courier Bulletin* (current printing of courier flights WORLDWIDE.
- Fax-on-Demand service for daily updates on courier available flights.
- On-Line courier & consolidator flight availability.

> **International Features**
> 8 South "J" Street
> P.O. Box 1349
> Lake Worth, FL 33460 USA
> (407) 582-8320

Consumer Reports Travel Letter
$37 for 12 issues and worth every penny.

> **Consumer Reports Travel Letter**
> Subscription Department
> P.O. Box 51366
> Boulder, CO 80321-1366

International Travel News
Monthly magazine for the international traveler. Super news source and communication medium for business and/or pleasure travelers to foreign destinations outside of North America and the Caribbean. $16 dollars per year.

International Travel News
520 Calvados Ave.
Sacramento, CA 95815
(800) 486-4968

Jesse Limited Flight Tote
Doubles as a shoulder bag with a detachable strap or
simply unzip the back panel to reveal adjustable, padded
shoulder straps to carry it as a backpack. Maximum
allowable size carry-on allows for overstuffing. ($70 -
Black, Maroon, Gray, Blue.)

> **Jesse Ltd.**
> 305 W. Crockett
> Seattle, WA 98119
> **1-800-274-3048**

Travel Bookstores
The best place for travel books, maps and accessories.

Int'l Assoc. Medical Assistance to Travelers
(716) 754-4883

State Department Travel Advisory Hotline
(202) 647-5225 or (202) 647-5226
Call for up-to-date travel advisory.

Centers for Disease Control and Prevention Hotline
(404) 332-4555 (404) 639-2572
Lists areas where there are outbreaks of disease.

Air Travel Complaints
Department of Transportation (202) 366-2220
Aviation Consumer Action Project (202) 833-3000
FAA Consumer Hotline (800)FAA-Sure

Travel Agent Complaints
American Society of Travel Agents (703) 739-2782
U.S. Tour Operators Association (212) 944-5727

BIBLIOGRAPHY

Air Canada, *Aeroplan*, Canada.

Air Courier Bulletin, Byron Lutz, 1993

Alaska Airlines, *Mileage Plan*, USA, 1991.

America West Airlines, *Flight Fund*, USA, 1989.

American Airlines, *Advantage*, USA, 1992.

Continental Airlines, *One pass*, 1991.

Daily Breeze, PARADE Magazine- *What You Must Know Before You Fly*, Sunday, June 14, 1992.

Delta Airlines, *Frequent Flyer*, USA, 1992.

European Travel Network,*Travel Card Program, 1992.*

IBC Pacific, *The Casual Courier*, 1993.

Lantos, *Travel Unlimited*, 1992.

Monaghan, Kelly, *The Insiders Guide To Air Courier Bargains*, Inwood Training Publications, N.Y., 1992.

Northwest Airlines, *World Perks*, USA, 1992.

Perkins, Ed, et al, *Consumer Reports Travel Buying Guide 1992*, Consumer Reports Book, Yonkers, New York, 1992.

The Shoestring Traveler, Byron Lutz, 1993

TWA, *Frequent Flight Bonus*, 1992.

United Airlines, *Mileage Plus*, U.S.A., 1991.

USAir, *Frequent Traveler*.

U.S. Department of the State
Foreign Entry Requirements February, 1993

U.S. News & World Report, *Travel- A Guide To Cheap Airfares*, June 29th, 1992.

ORDER FORM

AIRFARE SECRETS EXPOSED

PLEASE SUPPORT YOUR LOCAL BOOKSTORE! We at UIC and Sandcastle Publishing and Distribution are committed to supporting local bookstores. If you wish, you may write or fax your order directly to us.

POSTAL ORDERS: Universal Information Corp., Customer Service—Order Dept., 2812 Santa Monica Blvd. #203, Santa Monica, CA 90404

PHONE/FAX MASTERCARD/VISA ORDERS:
Sandcastle Publishing & Distribution   (213) 255-3616
Please fill out form and have your card # and expiration date available.

DISTRIBUTION TO THE BOOKTRADE:
Sandcastle Publishing & Distribution   (213) 255-3616
Competitive discount schedule, terms & conditions. Will work from official store purchase orders. STOP orders OK. If CA business, resale number must accompany order.

TRAVEL BOOKS—ALL BUDGETS, MANY SPECIALTIES:
Traveler's Bookcase (213) 655-0575   1-800-655-0053 (outside CA.)
California Map & Travel   (310) 829-6277

Please send the following books. I understand that I may return any books in unmarked and resalable condition for a full refund—for any reason, no questions asked within 7 days of receipt of the book.

Number of Books Ordered: _____ Cost of Books: $16.95 x _____ = _____
Sales Tax: = _____
  Please add 8.25% sales tax for books shipped to a California
  address. ($1.40 for one book, $2.80 for two, etc.)
Packaging/Shipping: $3.75 for first book plus $1.25/add'l book   = _____
TOTAL   = _____

Please send my order to:

Name _____
Address _____
City _____ State _____ Zip Code _____
Daytime Phone Number with area code first _____